Brutal

NABILA SHARMA

Brutal

The heartbreaking true story
of a little girl's stolen innocence

Certain details, including names, places and dates,
have been changed to protect the author's privacy.

HarperElement
an imprint of HarperCollins*Publishers*
77–85 Fulham Palace Road,
Hammersmith, London W6 8JB

www.harpercollins.co.uk

and HarperElement are trademarks of
HarperCollins*Publishers* Ltd

First published by HarperElement 2012

1 3 5 7 9 10 8 6 4 2

A catalogue record of this book
is available from the British Library

ISBN 978-0-00-743849-5

Printed and bound in Great Britain by
Clays Ltd, St Ives plc

MIX
Paper from
responsible sources
FSC™ C007454

FSC™ is a non-profit international organisation established to promote
the responsible management of the world's forests. Products carrying the
FSC label are independently certified to assure consumers that they come
from forests that are managed to meet the social, economic and
ecological needs of present and future generations,
and other controlled sources.

Find out more about HarperCollins and the environment at
www.harpercollins.co.uk/green

Contents

Prologue

I'm running around the garden in the sunshine. My brother turns to throw a red rubber ball towards me and I watch as it sails high up into the air. I stretch up my hands to try and catch it and, as I do, the sunshine blinks between my fingertips. It's a hot day and I can feel the sun baking my skin.

My dolls are sitting in a neat line in their pram. I've brushed their long glossy hair and dressed them in nice clothes and they look beautiful. Their hair isn't as long as mine, though. Mine stretches below my bottom and attracts comment wherever I go. 'Isn't she lovely?' they say. 'What a beauty!'

Maybe that's why the new imam at the mosque singles me out from the start. 'You're a pretty one,' he says, and asks me to help with the cleaning. I feel very proud. He's a strange-looking man, with his freckles and protruding belly and the funny sarong he wears, but he's the imam, the leader of our community, the one all the parents want to impress. The other girls are jealous of the attention he pays me.

Every evening after school I go to the mosque for lessons with seventy other children. We all line up to shake the imam's hand and say 'Salaam alaikum', to which he replies 'Alaikum salaam'. But one night as he holds my hand, he does something odd. He strokes the inside of my palm with his index finger, wiggling it around, tickling me. I'm confused. Should I do the same thing back? Then he jabs his finger hard into my hand, as if to make a point.

I watch carefully as he shakes hands with the other children and I don't think he does the funny handshake with them.

It's on my mind as I play in the garden. Why me? There are times when I'm not sure what to make of it. I'm only seven. I feel like I've been chosen for something. But I don't know what.

Chapter 1

The Girl with Ribbons in Her Hair

I slipped on my shoes without stopping to fasten them, opened the back door and shot straight out into the back garden. My brother Asif was holding my favourite doll by the hair, swinging her round like a helicopter.

'I'll get you!' I shouted crossly, waving my tiny fist in the air.

The shoes slopped off my heels with every step I took, slowing me down.

'Give me my doll!' I demanded as I tried to catch him.

'Nope,' Asif teased.

'Give her back now or ... or ...' I couldn't think of a strong-enough threat.

'Or what?' he challenged.

'I'll tell Mum.'

'Oooh, I'm really scared,' Asif laughed. The doll spun faster and faster around his head, her arms and legs splayed out. She was already naked and muddy from being kicked around the garden.

With all my might I stretched up on tiptoes to try and grab her, but it was no good. Asif was much taller than me. I hated my brothers. They were mean to me. Why didn't I have a sister instead?

I rubbed my eyes and began to sob.

'Anyway, it's only a stupid doll,' Asif teased, knotting her hair between his fingers. He was eight years old to my five, and an expert at winding me up.

The sky had clouded over and it began to rain. I felt utterly miserable as the drizzle fell on my upturned face.

'Nabila!' Mum's voice called suddenly from the back door.

Asif froze. Had Mum spotted him tormenting me from the back window? He dropped the doll guiltily on the ground and took a giant step away.

I seized the moment and, scooping her into the safety of my arms, surveyed the damage. Her ice-blonde hair was knotted and ratty and her face was caked in mud. With the sleeve of my dress I wiped a big dollop of mud from her forehead.

'There, that's better, isn't it?' I soothed, rocking her in my arms.

Asif was still watching the back door to see if Mum was about to come storming out, so I grabbed my chance and gave him a swift kick on the leg.

'Oww,' he groaned, rubbing his shin bone.

'Nabila!' Mum called again, her voice impatient. 'Come in now. I need to do your hair!'

I rolled my eyes skywards and called, 'Okay, coming!'

Asif's face broke into a sarcastic smile. 'Go on then, pretty little girl,' he teased in a whiny voice. 'Hurry up and get some greasy oil in your stupid hair!'

I stuck my tongue out at him, and hurried inside to where Mum was waiting.

The room was too hot. She had the gas fire on full blast and the flames flickered from yellow to blue. I thought how pretty they looked as they danced across the front of the fire.

The room smelled of coconuts. Mum had melted some coconut oil in a little silver bowl balanced on top of the gas fire. She swore by it because she'd heard that it made your hair thick and strong but, more importantly, that it made it grow even faster. Mum was obsessed with my hair.

'It's your crowning glory, Nabila,' she insisted. 'You must look after it.'

I hadn't had my hair cut since the day I was born and by the time I was five it hung down below my bottom. When I sat on the floor the ends would flick out along the carpet like black spiders' legs trying to crawl away from me. Every day Mum would oil and plait my hair in front of the fire. I hated it because it always took ages, and when she pulled too hard it hurt. Sometimes it felt as if she was sticking a thousand pins into my scalp as she tugged and plaited it all with ribbons.

Everyone noticed my hair, and the comments were usually admiring – but not always. One day, I was walking down the street holding Mum's hand when a lady passed us. As soon as she saw the plaits swishing around my bum, she stopped and did a double-take.

'It's cruel letting a child wear her hair so long!' she exclaimed to Mum. 'It must be so much work.'

Mum just stuck her nose in the air as if she didn't care. I don't know what the woman's problem was. I loved the fact my hair was so long I could sit on it. It made me feel special, like Rapunzel.

It wasn't just my hair Mum fussed over; she also made all my clothes herself. She shopped around for different fabrics and ran them up into outfits on her little sewing machine. I had tops and trousers in every colour of the rainbow. My favourite dress was a sunshine yellow one with a zig-zag red trim along the bottom of the hem. It was bright and beautiful.

Whenever she did my hair Mum would be sure to match the colour of the ribbon with the outfit I was wearing. She threaded the ribbons inside my plaits and the colour streaked through, making them look even longer.

Dad said that the reason why Mum dressed me like a doll was because she'd waited so long for a little girl. When I was finally born, she couldn't believe it. She had almost died during the pregnancy. She'd been working in our family's shop when she began to feel really ill and collapsed. Dad called for the doctor, who diagnosed tuberculosis – a horrible word that stuck in my head. The GP warned them that even if the baby was born alive, it would be horribly deformed.

In fact, the doctor was so convinced of this that he insisted on being present at my birth, ready to comfort my parents when they saw me. But against all odds I arrived perfectly healthy and with a full head of black hair!

Dad was so delighted that he jumped around the room with joy. Mum just sat and wept quietly.

'Why was she sad?' I asked.

Dad shook his head. 'Not sad, Nabila. She cried because she was so happy. You were all she ever wanted.'

He explained that he'd chosen the name Nabila as soon as the midwife placed me in his arms. 'We chose it because it means happiness, and after your four brothers your mum was happy to finally have her little girl.'

He told me that I'd had a fifth brother called Aaban, but he'd died when he was only six hours old. His lungs weren't strong enough to breathe outside Mummy's tummy. My parents held his tiny hand and cried whilst they watched his life ebb away. Dad said losing Aaban broke Mum's heart, but that I'd mended it.

'That's why you are so precious to us. You mean the world to us,' he said, kissing me tenderly on my forehead.

My father's family had rescued Mum from a horrible life as an orphan back in Pakistan. Her mother had died when she was three years old, then her dad died when she was seven. My mother, whose name was Shazia, her brother Sawad, then aged twelve, and her nine-year-old sister were split up and farmed out to different relatives. Mum was taken in by her grandmother but the family were cruel and treated her like a slave. My dad's mother, who lived close by, realised what was going on and took Shazia in and gave her shelter, then my dad, Mohammed, the eldest son of the family, decided to marry her when he was twenty-eight and she was just thirteen years old.

I loved hearing the story of how my parents met. I imagined Dad as a dashing prince, saving Mum from her wicked relatives.

Dad decided to move to England to make a better life for his family. He told me he'd driven all the way to Britain from Pakistan in his car.

'I did it for me, your mum – all of us.'

He only stopped driving when he needed to sleep, except from time to time he had to stop and do some work so that he could afford another tankful of petrol.

I shut my eyes and tried to imagine my dad driving across the desert in his battered old car, like Lawrence of Arabia. It all seemed very exciting.

It took him almost six months to make the journey but he finally arrived in England at the beginning of the 1960s.

'Things were very different then,' he told me, his eyes widening at the memory. 'Women wore these very short skirts, and men – well, they wore their hair really long, like girls!'

I pulled at my own hair. 'What, like mine?'

'No, not as long as yours, but too long for a man. I'd never seen anything like it!'

Eventually, when he'd saved up enough money, Dad bought a shop in the Midlands, a typical grocery store with a butcher's shop at the back. He could turn his hand to most things, but he was a particularly skilled butcher.

Mum gave birth to my eldest brother Habib in 1968; he was followed by Saeed, Tariq and Asif, then I came along in 1976.

Habib was a typical eldest brother, eight years older than me but it might as well have been twenty. He was bossy and always telling me what to do. I hated Habib. He was moody and mean. He resented being the oldest because it meant he had to help more around the house and, in particular, he was often told to babysit for the rest of us.

Each night, Mum would chop and prepare all the food in the flat above the shop. We spent most of our time up there as youngsters, while Mum and Dad were working downstairs. At mealtimes, Habib had to turn on the cooker and heat up the food Mum had prepared earlier. It was his job to feed us.

'You should be the one cooking,' he complained to me. 'You're the girl, not me. This is a girl's job.'

That's how Habib was. He was clever and he knew it, but he also thought he was too important to look after the rest of us.

My second-eldest brother Saeed was a year younger than Habib, but he wasn't as smart. Saeed was good with his hands. He loved taking things apart just to see how they worked. One day he took one of my dolls to bits. First he pulled her head off and then her arms and legs until there was nothing left apart from a stumpy body. He tried to put her back together again but it didn't work so she remained an amputee.

He did this with all our toys and his own as well, which made my parents despair. When we were older and got bikes of our own we didn't dare leave them in the garden in case Saeed got his hands on them.

Tariq was the tough one, a typical boy, who used to beat me up all the time. He loved to fight and nothing or no one would ever be able to hurt him back. He was mad on wrestling and boxing and used me as his very own punchbag.

'Just stand there while I hit you,' he instructed.

'But I don't want to be hit. You'll hurt me!'

'I need to practise my moves and if you don't stand still I'll hurt you more.'

Seconds later I was lying in a crumpled heap on the floor, with Tariq standing over me.

'Get up, Nabila. I need to do it again.'

Sometimes he was so rough that he crossed the line and our so-called 'play fighting' became something more akin to torture, with me as the unwilling victim.

Asif was my youngest brother, and although he teased me constantly he was also the kindest one. There were only three years between us so we often played together, which annoyed Habib no end. He teased Asif for playing with a girl, but secretly I think he was jealous of our friendship because no one liked Habib.

I adored Asif. He was my favourite brother, and even if he teased me he always stuck up for me if need be. We spent lots of time together, making up games. My favourite was one in which Asif pushed me round the garden in my dolls' pram, like a baby. We'd giggle away until we felt sick.

As we grew older, though, Asif began to spend less and less time with me. He discovered football, his head was turned and he was off, leaving me far behind.

Our house was just a few streets away from my parents' shop. We'd moved there not long after I was born so that we'd have more room, but it was still small and cramped inside. There were three bedrooms upstairs but one was used as a storage room and was constantly piled high with boxes of stock from the shop. My parents slept in the second bedroom and my brothers shared the third. The boys had the biggest room, but with four of them sleeping in two double beds they needed it.

I slept in a little bed in my parents' bedroom. My dad worked in the shop by day and had a job as a labourer at night to supplement his income. They were building a new shopping centre on the other side of town and Dad was paid to drive a big bulldozer. It was his job to dig out all the soil so that building work could begin. It meant he got hardly any sleep, just sneaking a nap here and there when the shop was quiet.

Even though he was exhausted, Dad would always spend at least quarter of an hour playing with me when he got home from his night shift. I'd roll about on the floor as he tickled my tummy and sometimes I'd giggle so much I'd feel sick. Then he would scoop me up in his big strong arms for a cuddle and call me 'Baby'. It was his nickname for me because I was the baby of the family – his baby girl.

With Dad away at work most nights, I'd sneak into their double bed and snuggle up to Mum. I'd curl in tight, wrapping my arms around her waist and absorbing the heat from her sleeping body. It made me feel warm and safe to be next to her, although I was always closer to Dad when he was there. I was a real daddy's girl.

Maybe one reason I wasn't closer to Mum was that her English wasn't very good when I was small. She spoke to us in a mixture of her native Urdu and pidgin English, and while I understood most of what she said, I spoke only a few words of Urdu myself. Sometimes her lack of English made her struggle when she was serving in the shop so when I was five Dad suggested that she enrol in a night class at my infant school and learn the language properly. She improved a lot after that and would practise in front of customers, but if she went wrong or was lost for the right word, she'd call to Dad or one of my brothers for help.

Our grocery store sold staples like milk, bread, cigarettes and canned goods, as well as meat. We never stocked fruit and veg. I think Dad had an arrangement with the greengrocer next door that we wouldn't encroach on his trade.

I loved the fact that my parents ran their own shop because of the extra perks. When Mum and Dad weren't looking, my brothers would make me sneak downstairs and steal sweets from the front counter. One afternoon, just after locking-up time, we were in the rooms above the shop when Tariq told me I had to go and get some chocolate bars.

'Go on,' he hissed, giving me a jab in the ribs.

My heart was in my mouth as I crept silently downstairs, being careful to avoid the second-bottom step because it always creaked if you stood on it. At that moment I heard a noise above me and froze in my tracks. It was the sound of the toilet being flushed. Dad must be in there. I waited until I heard his heavy footsteps move into the living room. My heart pounded in my chest as I tiptoed over to the counter and grabbed as many chocolate bars as I could. I pulled up my trouser legs and wedged four or five bars in the top of each sock. With that I sneaked back upstairs, walking with difficulty. When I finally made it back to the room I was welcomed as a hero.

'Brilliant! What did you get?' Saeed said, grabbing at my leg.

'Wait a minute,' I said, slapping his hands away. 'Let me get them out first.'

'Yuck, I'm not eating them. They've been near her smelly feet.' Tariq stuck his fingers down his throat in a gagging motion.

'Fine, I'll have yours then!' Asif said, quick as a flash.

'Sssh,' Saeed whispered dramatically, putting his finger to his lips. 'Habib will hear, and if he does we'll all be for it.'

Habib was supposed to be looking after us and he'd have got into trouble if I'd been caught. Tariq and Asif shared the chocolates between them and all they gave me for my trouble was a Curly Wurly, but at least I'd earned their respect. Maybe having a little sister wasn't so bad after all.

This became a regular occurrence and I'm sure that after a while Mum and Dad must have sussed out what we were up to, but nothing was ever said.

The butcher's area at the back of our shop was always a hive of activity. Dad would take delivery of halal meat from the local slaughterhouse and I'd watch with morbid fascination as he chopped off animals' wings and limbs using special meat cleavers and razor-sharp knives. The sound of metal hitting the wooden chopping block used to make me jump. What wasn't chopped up was minced, using a large stainless-steel mincing machine. Dad's meat cuts were legendary and people would queue from early in the morning to buy the best joints.

At night, he'd wearily pull down the shutter at the front of the shop and head for his second job on the building site. I'd usually only see him in the morning, when I got up for school, and he would just be getting in from work, ready to wash and start all over again in the shop.

Soon, the toll of having two jobs began to wear him out so he called his brother Kahil over from Pakistan to help in the butchers'. Mum would work in the grocery, while Uncle Kahil served and prepared meats in the back with Dad. It gave my father more time to rest and it also gave Kahil a better life. Like my father, Kahil settled in England. He married a girl over in Pakistan and brought his wife back to England. Soon, they'd bought a house and begun to raise a family of their own.

With the extra pair of hands Dad was able to get some rest in the mornings, but he'd have to be there by midday to cope with the lunchtime rush so he still only had a few hours' sleep. He worked five nights a week at the building site and seven days a week at the shop.

At home, my four brothers would constantly bicker and fight. Mum was usually ratty and exhausted. She'd shout out orders in Urdu and deliver slaps here and there as she tried to bring some kind of order to the household, but it never worked and that made her even more short-tempered.

On the other hand, our father never raised his voice to us. He didn't have to, because one look from him was enough to quieten even the fiercest argument. His kids were his life but he couldn't stand confrontation and discord. He was a peaceful, hard-working man, who took pleasure in watching his children grow and develop. The last thing he wanted after all the hours he worked was to come home to any kind of trouble.

I enjoyed looking pretty and liked all the nice clothes Mum made me, but my looks separated me from my brothers. It stopped me joining in their games, because they saw me as some stupid girly girl.

'Where are you going?' I asked Habib one day, as I watched him retrieve a bat and ball from a cupboard underneath the stairs.

'To the park to play cricket,' he snapped, his tone implying it was none of my business.

I screwed up my nose, annoyed that no one had asked me.

'Please can I come?' I asked politely.

'Girls can't play cricket,' he answered crossly.

I was furious and wouldn't let it go. When Mum heard us arguing, she left the pot of steaming hot curry cooking in the kitchen to come out to the hall and intervene.

'Habib, take your sister with you and look after her.
If she wants to play cricket, let her join in!' she scolded
in Urdu, no doubt seeing a chance to get us kids out
from under her feet for a few hours.

Habib's face changed. A mood descended on him like
a black cloud. Reluctantly he agreed to take me, but he
flashed me a filthy look. Having his little sister in tow,
trailing behind him, slowing him down, would mess up
his plans for the rest of the day. With my back to my
mother, I stuck out my tongue at him – but my triumph
didn't last long.

As soon as we arrived at the local park I was
dispatched to the far reaches of the grounds. It was a
baking hot day and the grass was dry and itchy under
my feet.

'Stand there and catch the ball if it comes your way,'
Habib instructed me.

I stood where I was told and my four brothers disappeared into the distance. I could just about make out
that the game was in progress but I was further removed
from it than a spectator in a back row seat at Lords
cricket ground.

'Hey, when's it going to be my turn?' I hollered, as I
stood hot and uncomfortable in the sweltering heat, my
brown leather sandals too tight on my feet.

'When we tell you,' Habib yelled back.

Soon the light began to fade and I still hadn't had a
turn. I wasn't wanted or needed there. Instead I stood,
lonely and left out, like a spare part waiting to be
collected on the way home. I learned my lesson that
day. If I wasn't invited, it was because my four brothers

didn't want their little sister joining in. My place was to be pretty, the shining trophy of the family. It was no use trying to be one of the boys. I was the little girl with the ribbons in her hair, and that's all I was good for.

Chapter 2

Living on Sikh Street

Our end-of-terrace house, a little red brick building on a corner, looked identical to the others in the street apart from the corner wall, which was crumbling in places, giving the neighbours a full view of our messy back garden.

Dad was always trying to lay paths or fix things up in the garden, but I liked the fact that there was no solid wall because it gave me direct access to the house of my friend Suki, who lived on the other side of the road.

From the outside our house may have been the same as the rest in the street but the family inside was different. We were Muslims living peacefully alongside our neighbours and friends, all of whom happened to be Sikhs. I wouldn't have even considered the difference if my older brother Habib hadn't pointed it out to me.

'Muslims and Sikhs hate each other,' he insisted one afternoon.

'Why?' I asked. Suki was a Sikh and we didn't hate one another. She and her family were lovely.

'It's tradition. It's to do with land,' Habib said, not really explaining. 'It's how it's always been.'

I shook my head. It didn't make any sense to me. 'Well, I think it's silly.'

But Habib wasn't listening. He'd already turned away. I didn't understand what he had against Sikhs. I liked to call our road Sikh Street because I went to school with Sikhs, our neighbours were Sikhs and my best friend was a Sikh. It didn't matter that we were Muslims. All I cared about was which dolls Suki and I would play with later that day.

Unlike our house, Suki's was a newly built four-bedroom detached house with its own garage. The garage door was white, just like the walls inside the house. Compared with the hustle and bustle and general chaos of my own home, Suki's felt like heaven. It was clean and clear inside, with hardly any furniture. I was used to a cluttered house full of storage boxes from the shop, but Suki's had what seemed to me like acres of space.

There was a garage built on the side of the house but the family didn't keep a car in there. Instead, they'd turned it into a special prayer room, which you reached through a door just off the kitchen. Suki's mother had covered the entire floor of the prayer room with white sheets. We'd sneak in there and I'd gaze at the musical instruments that rested at the bottom of the room by the window. There was only one window that over-looked the back garden, so it was nice and private. A huge picture hung on a wall. Suki said it was their God, but that didn't bother me, even though I was a Muslim. Suki's family were deeply religious but they were also very kind. They didn't worry about me being Muslim. It didn't seem to matter to them.

All of Suki's family played the instruments in the prayer room. Suki was learning the tabla, which was a small drum. My eyes lit up whenever it was time for her to practise. Her mum noticed and decided to teach me too. The whole family allowed me to bang the drums and pluck at the strings of the sitar, even though I couldn't do it properly and just made a din. I always loved being in their prayer room.

Unlike mine, Suki's family didn't eat meat, not even eggs, so I was fascinated by their food. Her mother would cook up dishes using lentils and other pulses, which didn't look very nice but tasted delicious. She spiced the food in a similar way to us, but unlike my mum, who tended to take shortcuts, she made all her own food from scratch, including pakoras and samosas.

Once when I was invited for tea Suki's mum was running late and didn't have time to cook. When she called us in to eat I was amazed to see plates of piping hot orange food, which looked like nothing I'd ever seen before.

'What is it?' I asked Suki, prodding with my fork at a round object coated in a thick gooey orangey-red sauce.

'What, you've never had this before?' Suki gasped.

I shook my head. I'd never seen anything like it in my life. My mum didn't cook Western food.

'Mum,' Suki called to her mother, who was still busy in the kitchen. 'It's Nabila – she's never had beans on toast before!'

I could hear Suki's mum chuckling to herself in the kitchen and I felt silly.

'Try some,' Suki urged, scooping a forkful off her own plate before cramming it into her mouth. 'Hmmm, it's lovely.'

Reluctantly, I let the orange food slide into my mouth.

'Hmmm, it's lovely,' I agreed, copying Suki. I shut my eyes and allowed the creamy beans to slide down the back of my throat and found they were, in fact, very good.

At that moment, Suki's mother walked in. 'Everything okay?'

'It's delicious!' I said, licking the tomato sauce from my lips. 'Can I have beans on toast every time I come here?'

Suki's mother laughed and disappeared back to the kitchen.

After that, I loved going to Suki's house for tea and I'd always ask for beans on toast.

Back at home, Mum had endless pots of meat curry on the boil. There were always scraps of meat from the butchers' shop that needed to be used up. She made a legendary chicken curry, with lots of fresh coriander, and she would also cook curried lamb and goat. She was a pretty good cook.

My favourite dish was a gorgeous rice pudding, which I called 'Mum's rainbow rice'. I'd sit and watch as she mixed cooked rice, raisins, sultanas and coconut, before adding droplets of food colouring, using every colour you could think of. As she dripped them in one by one, the colours would bleed and be absorbed into each particle of rice, but before they became too blurred Mum would grab the bowl and flip it, mixing the rice in on itself. The colours would soak in and create what I called 'rainbow rice'.

At six years old, Suki was a year older than me, but our lives were almost identical, apart from our religions. Like me, she was the only girl in a family of four brothers, but, unlike mine, hers were dashing and exciting. They never cut their hair. Instead they wore it in a bun under a dark fabric turban. I'd never see her brothers brush or comb their hair and I was always tempted to peek under their turbans to see if theirs was as long as mine. Their hair was sacred to them and I understood that because I'd never had mine cut either. I sometimes wondered if I should put my hair up under a hat or something so I could be just like my friends.

Despite her evening classes, Mum still couldn't read or write very much English, but our Sikh neighbours took her under their wing and helped her. To our horror, they taught her how to knit and crochet, which meant we got even more hand-made clothes. Soon my brothers were moaning about all the outfits she was churning out at an alarming rate. They hated the fact that she made them all dress the same. Now, when they walked down the street everyone could tell they were brothers. There was no getting away from it. The stiff, brown

home-made shorts were horrid, but the itchy pullovers
were even worse.

'I hate these clothes! We look stupid,' Saeed moaned
to me in the garden one day. I covered my mouth to
stifle a laugh. I'd been wearing Mum's creations all my
life and, although my dresses were beautiful, they could
sometimes be a bit garish. Now it was someone else's
turn to suffer.

My mum was happy to have Sikh friends and during
the six years we lived in Sikh Street she became great
friends with Suki's mum, but at the same time she made
it clear to me that I would never be allowed to marry a
Sikh. In her eyes that would be wrong. It would cross
too many barriers. It seemed odd to me at the time that
mum could choose her own friends while, as a Muslim
woman, she couldn't choose her own husband, but I
always knew it would be the same for me. When the
time came, Mum and Dad would choose my husband.

The two women took it in turns to walk Suki and me
across the road to the local infant school. I loved school.
I was one of only a handful of Muslim girls but I was
treated exactly the same as everyone else. My school-
mates saw beyond my religion. Friendship was the most
important thing to us and I was sure that Suki and I
would stay friends forever.

When Suki's family went to visit the Sikh temple I
often went with them. The temple was a tall and impos-
ing building. The outside was painted bright yellow –
the colour of sunshine – and it had an Indian flag
hoisted high in the air, which flapped around proudly in
the breeze as if it was in the hands of a brave soldier.

There were ornate carvings on the outside, and a domed roof on top. I thought it was beautiful.

The Sikh temple was very different to the mosque where my father went every Friday. For a start, the women I knew didn't pray at the mosque, only men, but the Sikh temple was open to everyone. It was a large open room with white sheets covering the floor, like a bigger version of Suki's garage back at home. As with a mosque, everyone would have to remove their shoes at the door and cover their heads. We would then have to bow to the holy book, and make an offering of money. I never had any money but I would pretend, along with Suki. It reminded me of playing shops.

You could sit wherever you wanted but the women tended to sit together so they could all have a good gossip. Everyone knelt on the sheets to pray and the holy book was held high above our heads on a plinth.

My strongest memory of the Sikh temple is that it had a very happy atmosphere. The man at the front sang as he recited prayers and the worshippers would sing back and join in with him. I found it thrilling that we all got the chance to sing out loud, which we could never do in the mosque.

Members of the congregation brought food from home with them, and once the service was over they stood up and began to lay it out. It was served by both men and women. I thought how much Habib would hate it that the women and girls were treated the same as men and boys. For me it was fantastic, because not only did I get to sing and eat, but I also got to sit next to my best friend. I thought how much fun it would be to be a Sikh. After going to the temple, all I wanted to do was learn how to become a Sikh. Their lives seemed so pure and good. I loved being at Suki's house because there I could pretend to be one of them.

Then one day all that changed. Dad had been working long shifts back to back and the lack of sleep was getting to him. He realised that he couldn't go on working all day as a butcher and all night as a labourer. Something had to give, and that something was our home. By selling the shop and our old home, he would have enough money to buy a cheaper but bigger house somewhere else. He would keep his job as a labourer, but this way he would have more time to spend with us.

'Nabila, get your shoes on. Your father is taking us all to see a house,' Mum announced one evening.

'A house? Where?' I asked suspiciously.

'It's not far,' she explained, without giving too much away. No doubt she sensed that trouble lay ahead.

'But I'm not moving. I'm not leaving Suki and her family,' I wailed.

'We're only going to look at it. Now do as you're told, put on your shoes and get in the car.'

Dad never lost his temper but I could tell that he really wanted us to see this house, so I agreed to go.

Ten minutes later we arrived outside a huge Victorian house on a main road in a different area of town. It was smelly, noisy and dirty because the rush-hour traffic ran straight past outside. The patch of front garden underneath the window was tiny, not much bigger than a postage stamp.

'Let's go in,' Dad said enthusiastically, as my brothers and I stood on tiptoe, trying to peer through the dirty bay window at the front of the ramshackle house. A filthy torn net curtain hung limply in the grotty window as if it was trying to conceal the horrible contents within. The whole building looked broken and unloved, as if it had been deserted for years. It looked like a haunted house from one of the cartoons on telly. It made me feel scared just to be there.

'Who lives here?' my brother asked.

'No one,' Dad replied. 'That's why we've bought it!'

'Bought it!' I gasped, my mind racing with fear that I'd never see Suki or her family again.

Dad turned to give me one of his looks, so I fell silent. He put his hand in his coat pocket and pulled out a couple of large metal keys I'd never seen before; they were the keys to this haunted house. I wondered how long he'd had those keys in his pocket and how long ago he'd bought this awful building.

He placed the largest metal key in the lock and turned it. The front door creaked open to reveal a dark and damp interior. It smelt musty but it also smelt of something else – grass or plants. I was confused. As my eyes adjusted in the half light, I spotted the reason. There was a bush growing in a corner of the front room! The plaster had fallen from the walls and there were big chunks of it all over the floor. Instead of plaster, the walls were covered in twisted brown roots where a tree was sprouting from the middle of the wall! The windows at the back of the house were as grubby as the big bay window at the front but, unlike the bay, they were all cracked and broken.

'It's got a garden inside,' I whispered confidentially to my brother Asif, who was standing by my side, his mouth hanging wide open in horror.

The front room had no ceiling. Instead there was a huge gaping hole and daylight shone in. One of the upstairs bedrooms had a similar open-roofed arrangement. How could Dad even bring us to such a dangerous and horrible place, never mind buy it?

'It needs a bit of work,' he agreed, sensing our shock. He stroked the bristles on his chin thoughtfully as he contemplated the huge task that lay ahead. I looked back at him in astonishment. Dad was a builder but he wasn't a miracle worker!

My brothers were still wide-eyed, surveying the wrack and ruin that surrounded us.

'But I reckon with a bit of hard work I can do it!' Dad concluded. 'Look at all the extra room we will have.'

He told us later that it had been empty for almost nine years and I wondered why it had been so unloved. Was it haunted?

I hated the house from the moment I saw it. It was true there was going to be plenty of space for us there but all I craved was the comfort of our cramped terraced house back in lovely Sikh Street. I felt sad to be there and moving away from Suki. I wandered glumly to the window at the back of the house, which overlooked a huge back garden. I thought what an unhappy garden it was – unloved and abandoned. It was so full and overgrown that it reminded me of a jungle. I convinced myself that the grass was so long there must be snakes hidden in it.

I was still daydreaming, looking out at the long grass and the messy, entangled shrubs, when I saw something move between the leaves. They shifted and parted as a weight brushed against them. I rubbed my eyes and continued to stare hard through the filmy windowpane. At first I thought I was seeing things, that it was a trick of the light, and then I spotted it – a wolf! I screamed in horror.

It had a pointy nose, beady eyes and a long pink tongue, which dangled limply down from the corner of its mouth, covering razor-sharp teeth. To me, recently turned six years old, it looked vicious and hungry. I was convinced it was a sign – a sign that we shouldn't live in this horrible scary house.

'I've just seen a wolf!' I shouted dramatically. My heart was beating so fast I thought it would leap right through my chest wall.

My brothers came running into the room just in time to see the little 'wolf' slip back through a bush and disappear out of sight.

'You idiot, Nabila,' Asif said. 'That's a fox, not a wolf.' They sniggered amongst themselves, saving it up as one more thing they could tease me about.

I didn't believe him. I ran upstairs to find my parents and tell them all about the wolf, but they didn't take much notice. Mum was too busy with a tape measure trying to work out where her new bed would go. She was smiling to herself, delighted with all this new space she could fill.

'It's going to be great here,' she sighed.

But my heart was still in my mouth. This place was horrible. It looked like an old haunted house and now there were wild animals living in the garden.

'I hate it,' I sobbed, as Mum brushed my hair later that night back at our old home. 'Why do we have to leave here? Why do I have to leave my best friend?'

'But Nabila, you'll have your own bedroom,' she soothed. 'We'll have so much more space there. Won't that be lovely?'

She hoped that I'd take the bait, but I didn't. I didn't want to. I didn't care about having my own bedroom, even though I desperately wanted one – not if it meant leaving our lovely neighbourhood and moving to the horrible new house. I didn't want to live in a house with wolves in the garden. I wanted to stay here with my friends, the Sikhs.

But the decision had already been made. Dad started work on the new house and was gone from dawn till dusk trying to make it habitable. He did most of the work himself, although my older brothers helped to mix cement and paint the walls.

Three months later it was ready for us to move in. Dad stuck tape across the last cardboard box and gave it a satisfied tap. Our lives had been packed up and shipped out in a series of bags and cardboard boxes.

'That's the last of it,' he called to Mum.

I watched as Dad struggled out to the car parked in the street outside. He turned sideways as he shuffled the heavy box of breakables into the open boot. We were officially leaving. I couldn't believe it. This was the moment I'd been dreading.

Suddenly fear gripped me. I glanced out of the back window towards Suki's home. The back door was open. I saw my chance and ran all the way across the road to my best friend's house without looking back. Her mother answered the front door and smiled warmly as she looked down at me, breathless and seeming a little lost, on her doorstep. She invited me in and I saw my chance and dashed into the front room, whereupon I refused to move.

Moments later, my mother came to the door asking for me. Suki's mum ushered her in and pointed towards me, but I wouldn't budge.

'I'm not leaving, I'm staying here. You can't make me go!' I screamed, and began to sob.

The two women looked at me sadly. Suki came and wrapped her arms tightly around me and she began to cry as well. We didn't want to be parted; we wanted to stay best friends forever, just as we'd always promised to be.

'I want to live here with Suki and her family,' I insisted. Big, hot, wet, angry tears stung my skin as they rolled down my cheeks and dripped onto the carpet below.

'Nabila,' Mum tried to reason, 'come on. You can see Suki any time. Your father is waiting outside in the car with your brothers and if you don't hurry up we're going to be late.' She was beginning to lose her temper.

But I was adamant. 'I don't care. I'm not living there! I want to live here in this house. I love this house.'

I looked over at Suki, who was sobbing silently, and knew she felt exactly the same way. Then I looked up at Suki's mother with big, brown pleading eyes and she smiled gently. I hoped this might be like it was in the storybooks, that Suki's mum might offer to adopt me and save me from the haunted house and the wolf in the garden. I hoped that she would let me move in with them here, where I would live happily ever after. But instead she remained silent.

Mum tried to reason with me, but the clock was ticking and Dad was waiting in the car.

'Come on,' she said, taking my hand in hers.

'No!' I replied defiantly before launching myself at the huge stone fireplace. I stretched my arms as wide as I could so that I was gripping the corners of the stone. 'You can't make me!' I shut my eyes, hoping this would make my mother disappear and leave me here.

Mum tugged, but I resisted and clung to the fireplace like a limpet. Soon there was a right old commotion. Suki's brothers heard the racket and came running downstairs to see what was happening. By now, spurred on by an audience, I was in full flow. One of the boys started to giggle but he was silenced by a stern look from his mother.

Finally, Mum wrapped her arms around my tiny waist and gave one last big tug, which extricated me from the fireplace. The palms of my hands smarted where the stone had scraped against them. The rough edges had grazed them slightly and they were red and sore. I licked them, but that made them sting even more. This was the worst day of my life.

'Come on, Nabila, we need to leave now,' Mum said crossly. Then her voice softened a little. 'She can see Suki any time, can't she?' she asked Suki's mum.

'Of course she can.'

That day, I left our familiar old street and our wonderful friends behind. Little did I know the nightmares that awaited me at the new house, or the bigger demons that lay ahead, ready to snatch me from my happy and safe little world.

Chapter 3

The Wolf, the Witch and the Wallpaper

As soon as we arrived at the new house I shot straight to the back window to look for the wolf, but he was nowhere in sight. I was convinced that he was still there, his evil hungry yellow eyes watching out for me. He was hiding in the bushes waiting to attack me, I knew he was.

The grass was long and overgrown, just as it had been when we came to view the house three months earlier. Dad had done the most important jobs such as putting in new ceilings, replastering the walls and uprooting the plants in the living room so the house was safe to live in, but it was still a work in progress. The garden was the least of his worries so it remained overgrown. Of course, my brothers were delighted – a jungle was every boy's dream!

'Let's go and explore!' Saeed urged, leading the others through the back door, but I refused to budge.

'Nabila, go and play with your brothers,' Mum instructed, but I shook my head firmly. I was quite simply terrified.

'It's the wolf,' I whispered. 'I can't go in the garden because the wolf might gobble me up, just like the one in Little Red Riding Hood.'

Mum sighed and undid her coat, throwing it on the side. She knelt down beside me and held me by the arms.

'There is no wolf. It's a fox – a poor little fox. It lives in the garden because the garden is overgrown. It's probably hungry and just scavenging for food.'

'Well, I don't like it,' I said, folding my arms in defiance. 'I want it to go away. It scares me.'

At that moment my father walked into the room carrying a box.

'What's the matter with Nabila?' he asked.

'It's the fox in the garden,' Mum replied, rolling her eyes skywards.

'The wolf,' I corrected her.

Dad tried to reason with me. 'It's probably more frightened of you than you are of it.'

But I wouldn't have it. There was no way I was playing out in the jungle where there was an animal on the loose with big sharp teeth. No way.

'Okay, okay,' Dad said wearily. 'What if I clear the garden? What if we cut away all the long grass and trim back the trees, then will you play in it?'

My face lit up at his suggestion.

'I guess that's a yes,' he said, patting me on the head.

The garden was vast – around sixty feet long – but Dad and my elder brothers worked long into the hot afternoons, cutting back all the yellow-green wispy grass so the wolf had no more hiding places. All the big scratchy bushes and dark looming trees were cleared away until within a few days our horrible jungle looked more like a normal garden. My brothers weren't so happy but I was.

With the wolf gone, Dad separated the garden into sections. He grassed over the top bit so that we could play on it, while the bottom half was planted with lots of different kinds of vegetables: potatoes, carrots, tomatoes and cucumbers as well as a herb garden, where fragrant coriander leaves were grown to flavour Mum's chicken curry.

Dad also sectioned off another bit of the garden for Mum to plant her rose bushes. She loved roses and had a bush in every colour. However, the roses suffered from Asif's football practice. Time and again, Mum would scold him for kicking his ball in their direction, but by the end of the summer there were more rose heads on the grass than on the bushes.

'Goal!' He'd chant in jubilation as yet another flower fell to its death, and Mum would mutter in Urdu that she was going to strangle him.

One evening, I was looking out the back window when I saw Saeed and Tariq sneaking off down the garden to Dad's shed. It was still early but the summer was drawing to an end and the evening light was beginning to fade to a wash of inky blue. They looked stiff, awkward and suspicious, whispering to one another as they crept along. I slipped out of the back door and followed them, careful not to make a noise. By now they'd faded into the dusk, but I could still make out their shadows as the shed door creaked open and they disappeared inside. I was puzzled. Why didn't they turn on the light?

'How on earth can they see in there?' I wondered as I tiptoed closer.

As I neared the shed, I spotted something through the window at the side. At first I thought I was seeing things, but as I drew closer I saw it again – the small amber glow of a cigarette end. It burned brightly as my brothers took turns sucking the end of the cigarette and tried to breathe in as much smoke as they could without coughing. This was serious. Smoking was strictly forbidden. Saeed was still only thirteen and Tariq was eleven. If Dad caught them, all hell would let loose.

I was too scared to confront them but I kept watch, and every night, just before bedtime, I saw them nip down to the bottom of the garden for their evening fag. I think they must have stolen some packs of cigarettes from the shop before we left because I can't imagine where else they would have got them.

A few nights later I crept down towards the shed after them, but this time I couldn't see a glowing light. I ducked beneath the shed window and rose up on my tiptoes just enough so that I could peer through the glass but there was nothing, only darkness. Suddenly I felt a jab in the ribs. It was Tariq.

'What are you doing here?' He'd meant to whisper but it came out so loud it made me jump out of my skin.

I spun around to see him standing next to Saeed.

'I know everything,' I told them. 'I know what you've been up to – that you've both been smoking in Dad's shed. I've seen you!'

Saeed's voice was unusually soft and kind, but he gripped my arm tightly. 'You mustn't tell anyone, OK?'

I looked from Saeed to Tariq and thought of what Tariq might do to me if I told. I had no choice. I wouldn't utter a word about this to anyone.

'I won't,' I said. 'Promise.'

'Good,' Saeed nodded. My arm throbbed where he'd held it. 'Now get back inside the house before Mum notices you're missing.'

I never told a soul about my brothers smoking in the shed. I kept it to myself, a little secret between us, and that's how I learned that this was something I could do well. I was good at keeping secrets.

I missed Suki dreadfully at first, even though Mum arranged special play dates. Suki and her mother came to visit us at the new house several times, just to help me settle in, but the rest of the time I felt so lonely. My brothers had each other, but here, living on a main road, there were no other little girls to play with and I had no one to call on when I was feeling bored. At first I cried for my old friend almost every day but once I started my new school and made new friends things became easier.

After a few months I realised living here had some benefits. For a start, I had my own room and didn't have to share a bedroom with my parents any more.

My room was on the first floor at the front of the house, with a window looking out onto the busy road outside. If I craned my neck far enough I could almost see down the entire street in either direction. It was long and ruler-straight, with houses dotted along each side, then it came to an abrupt stop on our side of the road, where there was a petrol station at the end.

I loved having my own room, but there was one thing that I didn't like and that was the wallpaper. It was a horrible brown colour with a repeating pattern of a house with a boat alongside. Soon after we moved in my brothers told me a story about that wallpaper and managed to convince me there was something evil hiding inside it.

'There's a little witch who lives in that house and when you're asleep at night she comes out to look for you,' Asif told me.

'No, there isn't,' I replied.

But Asif was adamant. He was usually nice to me so I trusted him in a way I didn't trust the others.

'Yes, there is. See the little boat?' I turned my head to look at it. 'The witch gets into that little boat and sails away from the house at night and then she comes out of the wallpaper when you're asleep to get you!'

I tried not to, but I believed every word he said. I glanced nervously at the wallpaper and then back at Asif, who nodded his head grimly in confirmation.

At that moment Tariq passed my bedroom door and heard us talking. Asif beckoned him in.

'It's true about the witch in the wallpaper, isn't it?' he asked Tariq.

At first he looked a bit confused, but then he realised what Asif was up to and joined in. 'It's true. She wants to steal a little girl and take her back to the house where she'll hold you down and kill you!'

After that, I found it hard to sleep in my new bedroom. I'd waited all these years to get one, and now that I had I could barely sleep a wink. The wallpaper pattern swam in my thoughts whenever I closed my eyes and huddled beneath the covers in my bed. A seed had been planted in my mind and I couldn't stop it from growing into a new fear. Part of me knew it was silly but the other part was convinced that something evil was hiding inside that wallpaper.

I'd pull the covers over my head and pray that this wouldn't be the night when the witch came for me, captured me and took me back to her little house. All I wanted to do was run to the safety of Mum and Dad's big warm bed but they wouldn't let me. Some nights I lay awake the entire time watching the little house for signs of movement. My eyes focused on the tiny windows and sometimes I was convinced I could see something move inside. I held my breath, watching and waiting, and by morning I was exhausted through lack of sleep. First the wolf and now the witch – I hated this new house.

I begged Mum and Dad, over and over again, to redecorate my bedroom but I didn't dare tell them about the witch in the wallpaper in case they laughed at me.

'But you have the best room in the house!' my father protested. 'The wallpaper is brand new. There's a lot

more to be done in the other rooms before we tackle
your bedroom.'

Asif heard my pleas, glanced up from his bowl of
cornflakes and smirked. I shot him an icy stare. It was
all his fault that I couldn't sleep at night.

For almost four months I begged my parents to
change the wallpaper in my room. Eventually they
buckled and the day came to strip the dreaded pattern
from the walls.

'Goodbye, witch,' I whispered, as I helped Dad rip
the horrid brown paper off with a scraper. I couldn't get
rid of it fast enough.

'You're a good little worker,' he nodded
approvingly.

Dad erected a pasting table in the centre of the room
and uncurled a length of wallpaper with a pink rosebud
pattern. It was both pretty and girly, but then, after the
witch wallpaper, anything would have done.

'Better?' he asked, looking up at me for approval before he applied the first splodge of wallpaper
paste.

'Much better,' I smiled.

Afterwards, I adored my little bedroom with its
lovely fresh rose-covered walls. It was my own space
where I was free to be myself and escape from my
brothers. There was a single bed with white sheets and
a pink rosebud throw that matched the wallpaper. The
furniture was all painted cream and, for the first time in
my life, I had my very own wardrobe and dressing
table, where I kept my multi-coloured Asian glass
bangles and my little gold hoop earrings. There was a

large window at the front which let in the sunshine so my room always felt warm and happy. Maybe this new house wasn't so bad after all.

One day Aariz, one of our old neighbours from the shop, came around to inspect the new house and admire Dad's handiwork.

'Nice job, Mohammed,' he said as he spun around the living room taking in every nook and cranny. 'When you're finished here, perhaps you will come over and paint *my* house?' He winked.

'No, no, my friend. No more DIY for me. I've had enough to last me a lifetime!' Dad exclaimed.

Aariz had lived next door to our old shop for years before Dad sold it. The two men weren't great friends but Aariz was a little bit nosey and had wanted to see where we'd moved to and how well Dad had done for himself. Even though he liked to have a snoop around, I liked Aariz because he was friendly and kind to us kids. He'd always pop around uninvited when Dad was in and would often stay for dinner. Other than blood relatives we very rarely had visitors, but Aariz was different. I think this was because Dad was far too polite to tell him to go away. But Mum liked Aariz too, perhaps because he was always very complimentary about her cooking.

'You make the most delicious curry I have ever tasted, Shazia. It melts in the mouth,' he would say, kissing his fingertips.

Mum strove to outdo herself, wanting to make each meal better than the last. Sometimes Aariz's wife came with him and the two women would chat in the kitchen while the men ate alone in the prized front room. It was virtually the only occasion on which that room was ever used.

Even after we'd been living in the house for a few months, Dad continued to repair, nail and fix things around us so that it sometimes felt as though we were living in the middle of a building site.

One day Tariq pointed to some bags of sand in the hall and said, 'This is the house that Dad built.' After that it became a standing joke, but it was actually true. He'd plastered, painted and papered virtually every wall and ceiling, and repaired every floor throughout the whole building. All the rooms were painted the same colour – magnolia. In fact the whole house was magnolia, because Dad had a friend who worked in a paint factory and he smuggled out big tubs of the stuff, which he sold to us cut price.

My brothers shared two bedrooms between them, with a double bed in each room. They had no space to themselves and would constantly bicker and fall out. I think they were jealous that I had a room of my own. Perhaps that's why they made up the story about the witch in the wallpaper. On the other hand, teasing me was one of their forms of recreation.

Tariq was still up to his old tricks of torture but now he decided to make Asif his accomplice. One day Asif called me into the back garden. I ran out to him and saw Tariq standing at the bottom of the garden holding my favourite blonde dolly.

'What are you doing?' I asked, then I spotted a box of Swan Vestas matches in his other hand.

'It's an experiment,' Tariq announced. 'We want to show you what happens when you burn a doll.'

'No!' I cried, but Asif held my arms and made me watch as Tariq took a single match from the box, struck it and held the flame against my baby's long blonde acrylic hair. Within seconds she had become a dolly fireball.

'Now watch!' Tariq instructed as the flames shot high above her head. Soon she was singed, blackened and hairless, and the flames continued to lick and melt her pink plastic face and body. Tariq dropped the doll to the ground as her face began to contort with the heat. The flames had made her eyes droop and fold in on themselves. She looked horrible, like a monster – the stuff of nightmares.

I was sobbing, but still they made me watch until suddenly Asif had a pang of guilt and let go of my arms. He ran over and stamped on the doll to put out the flames, but it was too late. She was already melted and ugly, and now that he'd stamped on her her head was as flat as a pancake! She'd never be the same again.

'There,' Tariq smirked. 'She's all yours.'

I stood weeping over the charred plastic that had once been my doll. I hated having brothers, especially ones who ganged up on me like that. I never told Mum what they did to me. It wasn't worth it because she was always so tired and short-tempered that I knew she'd probably smack me for telling tales, then she'd punish my brothers into the bargain. Afterwards they'd hit me for telling in the first place, so all in all it wasn't worth it.

There was only one advantage to my brothers. Their mean reputations went before them, which meant that I was never picked on at the new junior school I had to start at after our move. I was seven years old when I enrolled there but Tariq was in the final year, with Asif a year below him, and having them there protected me. The bullies wouldn't dare pick on me for my super-long hair or my bright home-made clothes, not when they knew I was Tariq Sharma's little sister.

The school was housed in a modern, red-brick building just off a main road, with a large playing field at the back. It took both infant and junior schoolchildren, aged from four up to eleven. There was a big park just around the corner and, if we'd been good, Mum would take us there after school.

During my first year, she walked us to school every morning and picked us up at night. My brothers didn't like walking with Mum and me. Tariq complained that I wore the wrong shoes and that my coat was too big for me, but I think he was simply embarrassed to be seen with his little sister because it ruined his tough image.

Although we'd kept in touch with Suki and her family, the distance meant it was hard for us to stay as close as we'd once been. Our visits dwindled until we were only seeing each other on special occasions such as Diwali. I settled in well to the new school, though, and soon made lots of new friends. I was quite sporty and was chosen to be captain of the school netball team. As my confidence grew, I was picked for the hockey and rounders teams too. I loved all sports and would practise racing my friends across the school play-ground at lunchtime. I'd wear myself out, pushing myself to go faster and faster, and soon I was the second-fastest girl in my year, a title I wore like a badge of honour.

Far from teasing me, the other children seemed to admire my hair and often asked where I got my colour-ful clothes. Mum loved all the attention I was getting and it spurred her on to make even brighter and more ornate outfits. She loved the fact that I stood out from the crowd.

I felt happy and special – but what set me apart from my classmates also marked me out. Little did I know it then, but I was about to become a prime target. Before long, I would be punished for my looks by the most unlikely person anyone could have imagined.

Chapter 4

The

Mosque

I had just turned seven years old when I was told that I was to start going to the mosque. This was the age at which my brothers had started. I'd go every week night after school from five till seven in the evening, and I'd have to keep going until I had learned the entire Koran, which was a pretty daunting prospect. It was all part of being Muslim, though, so I accepted I had no choice. I told myself it would be exciting and different. I felt the butterflies fluttering in my stomach at the sheer thought of it, but at the same time it made me feel very grown up. It was a sign that I was growing older and wiser.

Besides, I was eager to learn the Koran. Muslims considered it the word of God and I knew that it was as important to us as the Bible is to Christians. My parents weren't particularly religious: Dad went to mosque once a week, at a mosque on the other side of town where he met his friends, but Mum didn't go at all. To me, learning the Koran was a challenge, something that I'd have to learn to be tested on later. I was excited about going to this mysterious new place with my brothers and without Mum and Dad. I resolved to try my very best at being a good Muslim. I wanted to make my parents proud of me.

Before I started, my father sat me on his lap. 'Nabila, promise me you'll work hard at the mosque?'

'Yes, Dad, I promise.'

I knew it was important to him and I loved my dad so much that I'd have done anything to make him happy.

None of my friends from school went to a mosque so they all thought it was very exciting, but because of this I didn't really know what to expect. Would there be handsome men dressed in lovely long robes like princes, waiting to teach us ancient religion?

I was nervous about the other children there. What would they be like? Would they be nice and friendly? Would I make more new friends? The more I thought about it, the more I wanted to start, until I was quite literally counting the days.

My brothers had been going to the mosque for a couple of years but they never talked to me about it. I wondered why. When I asked, Asif told me that they all hated going and I thought that was curious. But I was a girl and I told myself I was bound to enjoy it more than them. They hated everything apart from football and cricket.

Habib had been going to the mosque for so long that he was coming towards the end of his studies. He was fifteen years old and said to be a fine student. He'd read the whole Koran, and now he knew it off by heart. I heard him practising in his bedroom. I hoped that I'd be smart like Habib and that I'd be able to learn the Koran, just like him.

As the oldest, it would be Habib's job to walk us all to the mosque. I felt sorry for him sometimes because he spent his life babysitting for us. This time he couldn't object, though. I could spend time with my brothers and there was nothing they could do to get rid of me. This was a new chapter in my life and I planned to enjoy every single moment of it.

Before my first lesson at the mosque, Mum drew me aside and handed me a black cotton scarf. 'This is to cover your head once you go inside. You must remember to wear it whenever you are in the mosque,' she instructed. 'You must be modest, Nabila.'

I took the scarf and tied it the way she showed me so that it covered my neck and hair and only my face was showing. You had to do this inside the mosque so that you didn't attract men. All Muslim women did it. We were supposed to cover any part of us that might be deemed attractive. Mum had always made a huge fuss of my hair, so I understood that it was seen as something beautiful and, according to our religion, all beauty had to be covered inside the mosque. The scarf could only be removed once you left.

My mum didn't wear a headscarf at home, but she always wore one when she was out in public. Like me, she had long, thick dark hair. Some other mums were much stricter and made their daughters wear a scarf everywhere except in the family home, but mine didn't

care as long as I covered my head in the mosque. Mum's
scarf was hot and it made my scalp itchy so I decided
that as soon as I'd walked out of the mosque door I'd
rip it straight off my head.

She also explained that there was a special rule that
women and men had to be separated during prayer. She
said it was to prevent them being distracted by 'impure
thoughts'. My brothers told me it was to stop something called 'fornication'. I nodded knowingly despite
the fact that at just seven years old I didn't have a clue
what they meant. Judging by Asif's giggles, I assumed it
was something very rude.

School finished at three-thirty so we had just enough
time to run home and grab some tea before it was time
to go. Before we left home, I washed myself in prepara-
tion for prayers, being careful to clean my feet, hands,
face and body. Mum explained I had to be clean to pray
and that this was something I'd have to do before every
trip to the mosque.

That first evening she walked down the road with us.
It was a cold evening and the wind blew an icy chill
clean through me. I shivered and pulled my winter coat
tighter against my body.

'What's it like at the mosque?' I asked for the
umpteenth time, but my brothers seemed curiously
reluctant to say anything in front of Mum.

I knew I was to learn my lessons from someone called
an imam, so I asked what he was like.

'Very strict,' said Asif. 'He's quite scary.'

I guessed they were exaggerating and making it up to
frighten me, just as they had with the witch in the

wallpaper. I couldn't get them to say anything more, though, so I soon gave up trying.

The mosque was around half a mile away from where we lived on the opposite side of the road. Even though the road was long and straight, you couldn't see the mosque from my bedroom because it was too far and it was hidden by several roundabouts on the way. I'd imagined that it was going to be a big beautiful building, just like Suki's temple, but it wasn't. It was new and hadn't long been built. There were no domes or carvings on it. Instead it was a three-storey, white-painted building with a sky-blue front door, and it looked like any old office building. It stood between a house and a factory, just by a busy main junction, which was controlled by traffic lights.

As we arrived, the lights turned red and several cars queued up in a line. The faces of the white families pressed up against their car windows to gaze at the mosque as if it was a place of mystery. As I watched them, I thought to myself that I was just like the children in those cars – I didn't know any more about this place than they did.

I was looking up at the mosque when Mum tapped me on the shoulder and gestured towards my head. I remembered the black cotton scarf, which was folded neatly in my coat pocket. I pulled it out and shook it until it was fully open. The wind blew, making the cloth arch out like a mini parachute. I wrapped it snugly around my head, securing it with a fat knot under my chin. It was far too big, even though I had acres of hair, so I tucked it under the edges of my collar to hide the rest of my neck. I wanted to be sure to create a good impression right from the start.

My mother turned to leave us at the mosque door. 'Just do as your brothers tell you,' she instructed, before planting a quick kiss on my forehead, and with that she walked away.

I stood and waved after her, feeling forlorn. I'd been excited for ages about this moment but now, even though I was there with my four brothers, I suddenly felt very alone.

Habib sighed and pushed open the heavy front door. Saeed, Tariq and Asif followed him and then it was my turn. The door was too heavy for me to hold so it slipped from my grasp and came crashing to a close with a loud bang. The noise echoed around the empty building and Saeed shot me a look of disgust. I'd already broken the first rule – to be quiet – and I'd only just set foot in the place.

We were the first children to arrive that night. I watched my brothers and copied what they did. As soon as they were inside the hall they removed their shoes, placing them near the door. I noticed that they left their school socks on so I did the same and placed my black shoes neatly alongside theirs. I'd done this many times before at Suki's house and again at the Sikh temple. I hoped that the mosque would be as joyful as the lovely temple. Maybe there would be singing. If we were lucky, we might even get a bite to eat. However, as soon as I stepped inside the mosque and saw the dreary interior I knew this was going to be very different from Suki's lovely temple.

Inside there was a large open carpeted space and very little furniture. Long wooden benches had been pushed hard against the sides of the room and above them hung a long bookshelf, which contained all the children's prayer books. It wasn't a happy place like the temple; I could tell that this was a serious place – even more serious than the headmaster's office at school. Suddenly, I began to feel very nervous.

The noise of the heavy banging door had brought the imam down to greet us. He was a tall, gruff-looking man, smartly dressed in a grey tunic and trousers. Like us, he wasn't wearing shoes. He came towards us but there were no smiles or warm welcomes.

'Don't say anything, just follow what we do,' Habib hissed at me, and I did as I was told, terrified that I'd somehow get it wrong.

Habib straightened his back and shoulders and tried to look confident. He was the eldest, so he wanted to set a good example. He walked towards the imam, holding out his hand. I caught sight of his expression and he looked different somehow, as though he was a little nervous. This was maybe the only time in his life when Habib wasn't in charge. It shocked me. Habib wasn't normally frightened of anyone but he looked very wary of this man.

I remembered Asif warning me on the way there: 'You don't ever disrespect the imam.'

The imam took Habib's hand in his and shook it formally.

Habib spoke: 'Salaam alaikum.'

The imam's expression didn't change as he bowed his head politely and replied: 'Alaikum salaam.'

'What does it mean?' I whispered to Asif.

He leaned in close, trying to speak quietly, but his words carried across the mosque in a whispered echo: 'It's an Islamic greeting. It means peace be unto you.'

Habib shot us a sideways look, warning us to be quiet.

Next it was Saeed's turn to shake hands, then Tariq's, Asif's, and finally mine. I'd memorised the greeting but I was a shy little girl and frightened that I would somehow get it wrong. The imam sensed my fear and was kind towards me, and thankfully I didn't mess up the words.

Once we had all greeted the imam, Habib shepherded us to the side of the room and pointed at some prayer books that were stored in a pile on the windowsill.

'Pick up your prayer book,' he told the others. But I didn't know what to do – I didn't have a prayer book.

The imam came over. 'Just watch and follow what your brothers do,' he said gently in Urdu, but I still didn't know what to do about the book because their books all had their names written on the front.

The imam sorted through the stack of books on the windowsill until he found a suitable one. He pulled it from the pile and held it in his hands, flicking quickly through each page to assess how difficult it was.

'Here,' he said, 'use this one.'

I glanced at the book in my hands and saw it was written in Urdu. With the imam only speaking to us in Urdu and the prayer books all in that language, I would have to try to learn more of it. I knew enough to understand Mum when she was shouting at us in her native language, but now I needed to learn it properly so I could recognise Urdu words in books.

The book I'd been given seemed too childish for my age. It had pictures of people kneeling on prayer mats, a dog, a boy holding an apple, a boy brushing his teeth, a drawing of a cow, even a man banging a drum, but when I looked at the squiggles by the drawings they meant nothing to me. They weren't like the letters I'd learned in school so I couldn't spell them out. How would I ever understand them?

I was sitting trying to make sense of the shapes and words in the book when the mosque door flew open and crowds of children – around seventy of them – came flooding in. Soon the room was bursting with kids. They'd been brought in by a special mosque bus from different parts of town and they filled the hall. The noise was deafening, as each and every one of them began to chatter at the same time. Some went off to wash themselves before settling down so that prayers could begin. Suddenly the imam spoke and everything went quiet. A hush descended across the room, and now it was the silence that was deafening.

The new arrivals sat on the floor and waited to be told what to do. Each one had a prayer book in his or her hands. I scanned the faces. There were all ages here, with primary-school kids sitting crossed-legged next to teenagers. Some of the boys were already sprouting dark hairs on their chins and top lips and looked more like young men than boys. These children lived in a different area to me and my brothers. Everyone seemed to know everyone else. I felt like the new girl on her first day at school again. But then, I suppose I was. Suddenly I felt very small within this big crowd.

I thought of my mum back home, cooking in the kitchen, and wished she were here with me now, holding my hand like she used to do when I was little. Nowadays the only times she held my hand were when we crossed the road, or when I didn't want to leave somewhere and she was dragging me out. She wasn't an affectionate, demonstrative mother in the way that some of my friends' mums were. Dad was the affectionate parent.

The whole room stayed quiet while the imam took his place at the front. He knelt behind a small wooden table, which stood only inches from the ground, just high enough to get his knees under. I tried not to laugh. To me it looked like a little dolly's table.

The imam told us to read and memorise a page of the Koran. I looked down at the squiggles on the page in front of me and couldn't understand a word of it. Asif saw me struggling and shuffled in closer to help. He pointed at the picture and then at the word, reading each one out slowly so that I could memorise it. I tried my best but there was so much to learn that I didn't know where to begin.

Other than Asif, I didn't speak a word to anyone. I was scared but still a little excited. I didn't have any friends here but it didn't matter because I had my brothers and they would look after me. For the first couple of weeks I stuck to them like glue.

Later that evening, the imam handed me my very own Islamic prayer book, written in Arabic, Urdu and

English. I felt extremely important. Inside there were
prayers for everything: prayers for the sick, and prayers
for when you were travelling on a train, bus or ship. I
examined the list at the back of the book and saw there
was a prayer for sleeping time, a prayer upon awaken-
ing, one for leaving the house, one for entering and
leaving the mosque, even a prayer for going to the
toilet! My head spun with it all. How on earth would I
remember any of it?

Despite my worries, my first night at the mosque
went fine. Mum was waiting by the front door when we
got back.

'Well?' she asked. 'How did it go?' She pulled at the
arms of my winter coat, freeing me from the sleeves,
before hanging it on a nearby peg.

'It was okay,' I told her.

She looked disappointed. I think she'd expected more
but, to be honest, I wasn't sure what I thought of the
mosque. I hadn't really known what to expect, but
whatever it had been it wasn't like that. I suppose I was
a little disappointed. I'd wanted it all to be as happy
and joyful as it was at Suki's temple. Instead it had been
very boring and serious. Still, it was only my first time.
Perhaps it would get better.

From that day onwards, Mum decided that Habib
could take us to the mosque every time.

'Keep an eye on them all,' she instructed as we set
off. I glanced up at Habib and he didn't look happy at
all.

'I'm always having to look after you lot,' he moaned
as we walked along the pavement to the mosque. 'I'm

sick of it. Nabila, walk quicker,' he snapped, picking on me for no reason at all. 'We're going to be late at this rate. You don't want to make the imam angry, do you?'

Lessons started at five on the dot, and the last prayer was at seven, so Mum expected us back no later than seven-thirty.

When we were walking to the mosque without Mum that second day, my brothers told me lots of scary stories about the imam.

'If he gets angry then you'd better watch out!' Asif began.

Habib explained that the imam would think nothing of hitting the children, but it was always the boys, never the girls. He'd hit them with the back of his hand. During the first few weeks there I didn't see him hit anyone myself but I believed every word my brothers said, even though the imam remained kind towards me. He was so tall that he looked like a giant, with a long white beard and hands as big as a shovel. I thought how much it would hurt if he whacked you with those hands. All the other children seemed frightened of him too, so I was careful not to stand out in any way or do anything to make him angry.

One night when I'd been there for a few weeks we were all sitting reading when the imam walked up behind a boy.

'You've not been paying attention, have you?' he scolded.

The boy looked up from his book and flinched when he saw the imam standing over him. He nodded his head weakly. 'I have. I promise.' He was so tense and nervous that his voice cracked when he spoke.

I glanced round at the other children but they just kept their heads down, as though they were trying to make themselves invisible. I couldn't take my eyes off the boy. By now he was shaking. You could tell that the imam was furious.

'You stupid boy!' he shouted.

The boy's eyes were wide with terror. I gasped as the teacher raised his hand high above his head.

'No, please don't!' the lad pleaded. He cringed and raised his arms protectively.

I winced and shut my eyes as the imam brought his hand down hard, giving the boy's head a vicious swipe. The slapping sound made my stomach somersault with fear.

The boy cried out in pain, and when I opened my eyes he was spread-eagled on the floor.

'Sit up!' the imam barked loudly.

The poor lad tried to pull himself back up but he wasn't quick enough. The imam brought his hand down again, this time on the boy's back. He yelped in pain, like a puppy that had just been stepped on.

I looked over at the other boys, at my brothers, and waited for someone to say something, but no one did. Instead they all kept their eyes down, pretending to read their prayer books.

I wished I was brave enough to grab the imam's hand and try to stop him, but he was a stocky, scary-looking man and I wouldn't have dared. Instead, I sat there like a coward, with all the other children, and I stared hard at my prayer book. My hands were shaking so much that the book trembled and I was scared that if the imam saw them he would start on me.

'*Don't look, Nabila. Just keep your eyes down,*' I told myself.

But I couldn't help looking up at the boy, who had now pulled himself into sitting position. He was clutching his back and had tears in his eyes.

'Now read!' the imam instructed, pointing towards the boy's prayer book.

The boy nodded and pretended to read, but there were tears rolling down his cheeks. I could see them dripping onto the pages and I was shocked because I'd never seen a boy cry before. My brothers would argue and fight but they never cried; crying was for girls. I felt embarrassed and sorry for this boy. I wanted to go over and see if he was okay but I didn't dare move. Like the others, I was frozen to the spot.

On the way home that night, I asked my brothers about the boy.

'The imam beats him all the time,' Habib told me. 'He's slow. He gets things wrong and it makes the imam angry. And when he gets angry, he beats you.'

I saw an entirely different side to that imam who had been so nice to me on my first day.

'Don't worry, he won't beat you,' Saeed continued. 'He never hits girls.'

I breathed a sigh of relief. That was something at least.

'Have any of you been beaten?' I asked.

They all laughed as if sharing a special joke between them.

'Yes,' Habib replied, 'we've all been hit by the imam. But usually he just gives you a quick slap around the back of the head. That's why you must be good, Nabila. If you're not good you will be punished.'

I was terrified and decided that going to the mosque was even worse than going to see the headmaster at school; at least he didn't hit you.

'What do people's parents say?' I asked.

Habib stopped in his tracks and turned to me. 'That's the whole point, don't you see? They send us here to learn. If you don't learn, you get punished. If you are punished then they think it's for your own good. Everyone has to do what the imam says. All Muslims do. It's just how it is.'

'But it's wrong,' I insisted. Mum sometimes slapped the boys round the back of the head but they were just little slaps. She wouldn't hit them hard enough to knock them over. If she was really cross she'd slap me on the back of the legs, but she wasn't as strict with me as with the boys so that didn't happen very often.

Habib nodded his head. 'Maybe, but the imam is powerful. Everyone's frightened of him, even the parents. You must always do what he tells you.'

After that, I saw more and more beatings. Boys were pushed, shoved, scolded and slapped for not learning their prayers or just for getting them wrong. Thankfully, that particular imam didn't stay long. He left and over the next couple of months our classes were taken by lots of different imams. You never knew who would be waiting to greet you with the customary handshake when you arrived at the mosque. Maybe it's because it wasn't a very smart or prestigious mosque but they couldn't seem to find anyone who would take over on a permanent basis. At least the replacements weren't violent like that first one, but still I worried each time we got a new one in case he would be rough.

The novelty of going there soon wore off and it became somewhere to fear rather than enjoy. It didn't seem fair that after the school bell rang and all the other children were going home for a relaxing evening we had to go on to yet another, tougher school.

When I'd been there for a couple of months Habib and Saeed stopped going altogether. Habib had come to the end of his studies, while Saeed just made up his mind that he'd had enough. He'd always been a rebel and when he turned fourteen he decided he didn't have time for this nonsense any more. I was sure he'd get into trouble but my parents knew they couldn't force him to do anything he didn't want to do, so nothing more was said.

Now I walked to the mosque with Tariq and Asif, but before long an incident occurred that meant Tariq had to leave as well.

One evening he was caught talking when he should have been reading his prayer book. He was still so busy chatting that he didn't even see the imam approaching silently from behind. The slapping sound as the imam whacked Tariq across the head was so loud that it echoed around the room and made everyone look up from their prayer books. Tariq reeled forwards, almost hitting the wooden floor. I gasped because I knew Tariq.

He was tough and fearless and I was sure he'd fight back.

The imam stood there waiting for my brother to cower and apologise, but he didn't. Instead, Tariq got to his feet and squared up to the bully. The teacher was stunned. Tariq was tall for his age and had the build of a man. He refused to move but just stood there, looking the holy man defiantly in the eye. No one pushed Tariq around.

The children sat open-mouthed as they watched events unfold in front of them. They'd never seen a child standing up to an imam before!

Suddenly, the imam lurched forwards and slapped Tariq again. The slap was hard and was meant to make him sit down, but Tariq hit back with a punch that caused our teacher to fall to the ground, where he landed in a shocked and dishevelled heap.

The imam struggled to his feet and glared at Tariq, demanding that he sit down. Again, Tariq refused. He was furious, and I knew from past experience that he would fight to the bitter end if he had to.

The teacher glanced at my brother and then back at the rest of us. We quickly lowered our heads, pretending to read, because we didn't want to be next. The imam knew he'd been shamed in front of us all by a young boy. Tariq was only twelve years old but he was stronger than the imam and the man realised he was beaten. He pointed weakly towards the door and told my brother to leave. Suddenly, our teacher looked very old and pathetic. He looked like the school bully who'd just been beaten up by a new and stronger boy.

That boy was my brave brother. My heart swelled with pride.

Tariq shot the imam one last look of disgust before grabbing his shoes and slamming the mosque door behind him. He'd had enough of the beatings. He left that day and never came back again.

I thought the imam might call my parents to tell them what Tariq had done, but he didn't. Maybe he was embarrassed to have to admit he was beaten by him.

I missed Tariq at the mosque because, of all my brothers, he was my protector, the one who made me feel safe. With him around no one would mess with me, but now that he wasn't there I felt more vulnerable. I still had Asif, of course, but I wondered how long it would be before he grew tired of this horrible place. I had already grown to hate the mosque; to me, it felt more and more like a prison each day.

Chapter 5

Arrival of the New Imam

Just eight months after I'd started lessons at the mosque, it was announced that a new imam would be coming, a permanent one this time. There had been talk of it for quite a while. The current imam gathered us all one night to tell us and he seemed excited that the position would finally be filled and there would be no more chopping and changing.

To be honest, I didn't pay much attention. There had been so many new imams while I was there that it seemed this was just another one to contend with.

Meanwhile, I had found myself a friend at the mosque – a plain-looking but kind girl called Farqad. Her name meant 'star' and she was to become my star and shining light. Farqad had eight siblings, so she knew what it was like to be bullied by her brothers and we sympathised with one another over that. Farqad lived at the other end of town and came on the mosque bus. Asif and I always arrived before the bus, so I would save Farqad a space next to me. We'd sit at the back, along with some other girls, and chat until five o'clock when our lessons began.

I remember clearly the first day the new imam arrived. The evening light had begun to fade and the first chill of autumn was in the air. I was still wearing a summer jacket and wasn't quite warm enough. I wrapped my arms round myself to try and keep out the cold, but still I was freezing by the time Asif and I reached the mosque. Some leaves had fallen from the trees and they swirled and danced round my ankles. As I flung open the door of the mosque, the warm air inside hit my face. I glanced up at the clock. It would be at least five minutes before the mosque bus arrived.

I pulled off my shoes and placed them by the entrance, then walked into the hall and wandered over to the wooden bench. Reaching up, I flicked through the pile of books on the shelf until I spotted my own prayer book. I'd written my name on the front in my best twirly handwriting. Suddenly, I felt movement behind me and sensed that I wasn't alone. There was someone else in the room with me. There was a new smell to the place as well. Above the scent of dusty prayer books I could smell stale spices and pungent body odour.

I heard a noise behind me and turned to find a strange man standing directly behind me. He smiled when he realised he had startled me. It took me a few moments to work out that he must be the new imam. I felt awkward, not sure what to say. He grinned and opened his mouth as if about to speak to me, but just at that moment the door burst open and a horde of children rushed in *en masse*. The bus had arrived.

The new imam called for the children to sit down. I took my usual place at the back of the hall and beckoned for Farqad to come and sit beside me.

Everyone was quiet, waiting to hear what the new imam had to say. I studied him for a moment in the lull and decided he was an odd-looking man. His skin was brown but he had freckles across his nose and cheeks. It was the first time I'd ever seen freckles on an Asian face before and he stood out because of them. I tried not to stare but couldn't help myself.

Unlike the other imams he didn't wear trousers but a dark shirt and a white sarong, which was draped across his body and barely covered his legs. It was like a short skirt, and his thin hairy legs were bare beneath it. He had a bloated pot belly that strained against the fabric and gave him an odd shape. I tried not to giggle as he waddled across the hall towards us because he walked a bit like a duck and his huge stomach made him look as if he were expecting a baby.

Compared to the other imams, this new teacher was really scruffy. He had a long, straggly white beard, which trailed down from his chin to a wispy point at chest level. When he got close to me, I realised there were bits of dried food stuck in his beard, probably the remnants of his last meal. Didn't he ever wash? That would explain the stale smell that hovered around him.

He came over to the group where I was sitting, and when he knelt down at the little table in front of us his sarong rode up his legs so far that we could see his black underpants. We girls gazed in horror at one another. I thought how odd it was. The imam was the head of the local Muslim community – the most important man I knew – so it puzzled me that he had his underwear on display for all to see. Surely he must know that we could see his pants? How could he not be aware of it?

His voice was much softer than those of the other imams we'd had. It was a kind voice, slightly high-pitched but gentle all the same. I recoiled when I noticed his teeth, though. They were all discoloured and, when he came over to talk to us directly, I realised that his breath smelled very bad, as if something had died and was decomposing in his mouth. I guessed that he never brushed his teeth.

On the positive side, it was nice to see an imam smile. The others had been stuffy and serious but maybe this one would be different. I hoped so. He certainly looked different to the last imam, seeming almost jolly. I hoped his presence here would mean an end to all the beatings for good.

The imam told us a bit about himself. 'I have come from Bangladesh, where I still have a wife and two daughters.'

I smiled when I heard that. I was glad that he had daughters; maybe this would mean he'd be nice to the girls – although it seemed odd that he had left his family behind. My dad would never have done that. He was always telling us that we were his life. I was glad this imam wasn't my dad, but at the same time I was sure he would do fine as an imam.

As it was, he didn't really have much to do with the girls. We would just come in, sit down and wait for the lesson to begin. He focused more on the boys. He was stricter with them and, like the others before him, he'd tell them off for talking. There was more pressure on boys. It was always a boy who would have to lead the prayers. Girls didn't lead prayers. Instead, we were shoved at the back of the room, almost forgotten. We were there, but at the same time we weren't. We were part of the scenery – seen but not heard.

There were so many children in the hall that the imam spent the first couple of weeks learning everyone's names. He remembered mine quite quickly because I was the only Nabila.

Children were called up in pairs to read to the imam, and the first time he called Farqad and me, I was petrified. I had been having a lot of trouble learning the prayers because my Urdu was so basic that I didn't even know how to pronounce a lot of the words, and that really slowed me up. Farqad was much better than me and already knew lots of prayers off by heart. Even though the imam had been kind up until then, I couldn't imagine what he might do when I got a prayer wrong. I gulped back my fear, but thankfully, when we got up to his table, the imam chose Farqad to say the prayer and not me. She knew it off by heart and sounded word perfect to me, so I was surprised when he corrected her.

'Try again, you didn't say that bit quite right,' he told her.

Farqad looked worried, but she needn't have been. This new imam was a patient man. She repeated the passage in question and he nodded, pleased with her.

My heart was pounding. That meant it was my turn now and he'd find out I wasn't nearly as good as my friend. I didn't even understand the prayer, let alone know how to recite it. He'd lose his temper with me for sure. Tension mounted as I waited for him to speak, but his next words astonished me.

'Very good,' he said, looking at me. 'You've both finished, so go and sit down.'

I couldn't believe it. I'd got away with it. He wasn't going to make me read.

'You're so jammy,' Farqad whispered as we went back to our place.

A few nights later, when he did finally ask me to read, the imam sensed my fear and picked out a particularly simple passage for me to recite. I felt blessed. Everyone else got the hard stuff but I was given the easy bits. I was beginning to warm to this new imam – even if he smelt.

One day I got something wrong, but, instead of shouting and losing his temper as he had begun to do with some of the others, the imam corrected me gently and asked me to try again. He was like a breath of fresh air: nice to the girls and not nearly as strict with the boys as any of his predecessors.

But then things changed. A month after the new teacher arrived, we were reading our prayers one night when he caught a boy talking. The boy, who can't have been any older than seven, was scolded for fooling around when he should have been praying. To be honest,

I think he'd been pushing the boundaries, convinced that this nice new imam wouldn't punish him.

'You!' the imam snapped, pointing at him. The boy looked up.

'Stand up!' the imam ordered in Urdu.

The boy got to his feet.

'Now go outside,' he said, pointing towards the door. 'Fetch a branch from one of the trees. About so long.' He held his hands roughly a foot apart. 'Be sure to strip all the leaves off, then bring it to me.'

The boy was puzzled and so were we. For a moment he just stood there, thinking it must be a joke, but it wasn't.

'Are you deaf, boy? Go and fetch a stick *now*!' The imam's voice boomed across the hall. We were stunned because it was the first time we'd heard him shout.

The lad realised the teacher was serious, so he bolted straight outside to look for a stick. There were plenty of them to be found out there, because the street was lined with trees. A few minutes later he reappeared, bringing a branch with him. He'd done exactly as the imam had asked and removed all the leaves from it. It was smooth and thin and bendy.

'Now give it to me,' the imam instructed.

The boy walked over and handed the imam the stick.

'Sit down,' he ordered, and the boy obeyed.

We all breathed a sigh of relief. It wasn't much of a punishment; the youngster had just had a lucky escape.

The boy picked up his Koran, placed it on his lap and began to read. We all lowered our heads and did the same. The room was silent until, from nowhere, there was a loud whooshing sound. I looked up just in time to see the imam whip the stick through the air and crack it hard against the little boy's spine. A blood-curdling scream rang out across the room. Everyone gasped and stopped what they were doing. The boy fell heavily onto the floor in front of him, where he lay, winded.

The imam didn't stop at that, but continued to beat him hard. Again and again, that stick swooshed down as the imam rained blow after blow on the poor lad.

'You stupid boy!' he hissed. 'Why did you make me do this?'

'Please,' the boy screamed, 'please stop!'

I couldn't look. I held my hands to my ears, beneath my long hair. I couldn't bear to listen to the sickening noise as the stick continued to cut into the boy's flesh. I couldn't bear to hear his cries for mercy. I couldn't bear to look into the imam's face, which was half crazed with fury. It was terrifying.

The beating lasted no more than a minute, but it felt as if it had gone on for hours. My mouth was dry and I wanted to swallow but was too scared in case the imam heard it and turned on me. The hall was silent, apart from the boy's pitiful sobs.

He lay red and sore on the floor, alternately crying and gasping for breath. I'd witnessed a few beatings at the mosque before but never one as brutal as this. It was all the more shocking because it was so cruel and unexpected. Would he turn on me next? Were any of us safe?

I felt Farqad next to me. Without realising it, we'd inched closer together until my thighs were pressing against hers. I could feel her shaking and my own body was trembling with fear as we sat huddled together at the back of the hall. I tried to curl my body up into a small ball so that he wouldn't notice me and pick me out next.

I'd thought this man was different to the others, but it seemed he wasn't. If anything, he was worse. None of the others had hit children with a stick. I decided that I would always make sure I did everything he asked. I didn't want to make an enemy of him. I thought about what Habib had told me: that I must do everything the imam said, otherwise I'd be punished.

'Get up,' the imam shouted at the boy. 'Get up and carry on with your prayers.'

The lad whimpered as he pulled himself up from the floor. He struggled to sit cross-legged and let out a small moan as he tried to straighten his battered back. I wanted to cry for him.

Meanwhile, the imam continued to stare at us all. 'From now on, if you don't do as I say, this is what you'll get!' he warned.

Everyone looked down at their prayer books for fear of being singled out. The room was deathly silent, apart from an odd sob from the beaten boy.

I pulled my hair across my face and glanced at Asif. I wanted to see his expression to try and work out what he was thinking, but he was busily studying his prayer book. All the boys looked terrified in case they were picked on next. All I could see was a line of dark bowed heads.

I tried not to worry. This imam didn't pick on girls. We'd all be fine.

But what if the imam beat Asif like that? What would I do? I couldn't just sit back and let it happen – but I knew I was too much of a coward to stand up to the teacher. I prayed silently that Asif would stay out of trouble. In the meantime I'd get on with my studies, work hard and become a good student, then surely we'd have no trouble.

It wasn't long after this when Asif had his own announcement to make. 'I've had enough,' he told me as we walked home from the mosque one night. 'I'm not going back there any more.'

I looked up at him in astonishment. 'You can't just stop going!' I exclaimed. 'What will Mum and Dad say? What will the imam say?'

Asif shrugged. 'I don't care. The others don't have to go any more, so why should I?'

I grabbed at his arm, feeling desperate. I couldn't face going to the mosque on my own, without my big brother by my side.

'What about me?' I begged. 'You can't leave me.'

But Asif was adamant. 'What *about* you, Nabila?' He pushed my hand away. 'We've had to go there for years. Now it's your turn.'

'But I'm frightened. I'm frightened of the new imam.'

Asif looked down. 'I'm sorry, but from now on you'll just have to go on your own. Hurry up and learn the Koran, then you'll be able to leave, like us.' His voice was light as he wrapped an arm around my shoulder. I knew he was trying to cheer me up but it hadn't worked. I shrugged his hand away.

'Look,' he protested, 'I don't want to go to that mosque any more than you do. I want to go to the park after school and play football with my mates. But I've learned the Koran so I can leave. That's all you have to do.'

His words rang hollow in my ears. Going to the mosque would never be the same again, not without my brothers. How could they leave me there with a man capable of doling out such brutal beatings?

My parents weren't very impressed but they allowed Asif to leave. I appealed to Mum, trying to persuade her to let me leave as well, but she was adamant I had to stay. 'Nabila, you have to learn the Koran, and until you do you cannot leave. Your father and I won't allow it.'

I wanted to tell Mum and Dad about the boy who'd been beaten with a stick, but I knew it was pointless. Dad had often told us stories of the beatings he'd witnessed at mosques over in Pakistan. Both my parents had seen children being punished by imams over the years and they agreed on one thing: if the imam beat you, it was for your own good.

To make matters worse, with the dark winter nights drawing in Mum insisted that my brother Habib should pick me up on the way home. He had turned sixteen and started a business studies course at a nearby college, but he wouldn't always be able to get there at seven on the dot. If he was late, I'd have to sit in the mosque after the other children had left to wait for him.

'Do I have to?' Habib moaned to Mum, but she had made up her mind.

'Your sister is far too young to walk home alone in the dark!'

As for me, I'd just have to sit and wait for Habib. I knew he'd be bad-tempered because he resented having to look after me. Even though the imam was always nice to me, I didn't want to hang around there any longer than necessary. I soon found that Habib was always running late, so I'd have to wait for him night after night for anything up to half an hour. It was boring. All I wanted to do was get back quickly so that I'd be allowed to watch a bit of television before bedtime.

'I'm getting out of here,' I whispered to Farqad as we sat at the back of the hall. 'I just need to learn the Koran as quickly as I can, then I'll be gone. Will you help me?' I knew that Farqad was a quick learner.

'Of course I'll help,' she promised.

'Thanks,' I whispered. 'A couple more years and I'll be done here.'

I was lucky to have a friend like her. With my brothers gone, she and I could look out for one another.

To look at, Farqad and I couldn't have been more different. She was skinnier than me because although I was only seven years old my body had already begun to develop. I felt embarrassed because my tops were starting to strain where my breasts were growing. I was curvier than the other girls, with a womanly bum and hips, but I didn't like them. I wanted to be flat-chested like my friends. I hated having a big bum and would constantly pull at my trousers, trying to stop them showing my shape. I felt self-conscious and awkward. Before, it hadn't been a problem.

I was paler-skinned than most of the other girls at the mosque and I still wore bright, fancy clothes made by my mother. My hair was so long that it skimmed the sides of my thighs when I wore it down. With my clothes, hair and now my different body, I stood out. When I was younger I used to like standing out from the crowd, but not any more. Now it made me uncomfortable. People often told me I was beautiful but I didn't want to be. I wanted to be plain like my friends. I wanted normal clothes and shorter hair. I wanted to blend in, to fade into the background, to disappear.

Not only did I have to hang around in the mosque after prayers waiting for Asif, but Mum started to make me go there early as well. I'd come home from school and eat the tea Mum had made for me, then she'd shoo me out the door, with one eye on the kitchen clock. 'You've finished your dinner, so you might as well start walking to the mosque.'

'But Mum, it's only quarter past four!'

'You're getting under my feet. Off you go and put in some extra study for a change.'

There was no arguing with her so off I went, but it meant that I was sometimes getting there as much as half an hour before the other children arrived on the mosque bus. The imam noticed that I was hanging around before and after lessons and he suggested I could do some chores for him to kill the time.

I didn't want to get into any trouble – I'd been wary of him since the brutal beating – so I nodded and said I'd be happy to help.

'You could start in the toilets – they could do with a clean.'

Was this a punishment? Had I done something wrong? I wasn't sure, but I did as I was told and wandered off towards the downstairs toilets. They certainly were in need of a clean, since they were used day in day out without a regular cleaner looking after them. It wasn't a nice job but I knew what to do because I often helped Mum to clean at home. I soon realised that the imam would let me miss some of the lessons in order to get the cleaning finished, so that was worth it. I began to realise that, far from being a punishment, he had given me a special responsibility. It made me feel quite important. I was doing something for the teacher, something that made him happy.

After a few weeks, the imam asked me to clean the kitchen upstairs as well. I was a bit shocked about this. Above the mosque were the rooms where he lived, and normally children would never be allowed up there. But he was new and I thought that maybe he didn't know the rules, or maybe he didn't care. Whatever the reason, I didn't dare say no. Instead, I climbed the stairs towards the kitchen. As I did so, I became aware of him following behind me.

'OK?' he asked.

'Yes,' I replied in a quiet little voice, feeling awkward and self-conscious.

I stopped at the top of the stairs to let him pass. I didn't know where to go because this area was usually strictly out of bounds. The teacher chuckled to himself when he saw me hesitate and I felt my face begin to flush. He gestured with his arm, beckoning me to follow.

'It's just through here,' he smiled.

Once I was inside his kitchen, I realised why he'd asked for help. The place smelled of rotten food and filthy floors. Dirty plates were stacked high, with food smeared between them, and pots had burnt remains stuck to the bottoms. My task was to sweep, wash up and tidy everything away but I didn't mind because it kept me out of prayers. I just couldn't get along with them, no matter how hard I tried, and I hated not being good at something.

Some of the girls were jealous of my new duties. They knew that I'd been singled out to clean for the imam. A few asked if they could clean for him as well, but he seemed only to want me. My chest swelled with pride. I felt special and important, but my new responsibilities didn't make me very popular with the others.

One of the girls approached me: 'How come you get to clean for the imam and we don't? What's that all about?'

I shrugged my shoulders. 'I don't know. He just asked me,' I replied. That was the truth. I genuinely didn't know why I'd been chosen.

'Well, it's not fair,' she hissed, shooting me a filthy look.

I tried to ignore her. I didn't care what the others thought. They were just jealous. I fantasised that maybe I wouldn't have to learn the Koran any more; maybe this would be my special way of getting through my years at the mosque – I'd scrub and clean for the imam instead. I'd be like his little housekeeper, keeping all his things neat and tidy. He'd be pleased with me and he'd tell my parents what a good student I'd been, so I'd leave with flying colours and make Mum and Dad proud.

I genuinely didn't mind cleaning. I was quite happy dusting, wiping and polishing things. It was like playing at houses, only this time it was for real. Whenever I finished my task for the day, I'd proudly wait for the teacher to come and inspect my work. I'd always make sure that the sinks, toilets and kitchen worktops were gleaming.

'A great job,' the imam nodded in approval. 'You're a good little worker, Nabila. Keep it up!'

I felt my face flush with pride. I was so happy I thought my heart would burst. I wasn't quick at learning the Koran, but as long as I kept the kitchen and the toilets clean, the imam would be pleased and I would do well here. And that's all I wanted: to be a good little Muslim girl.

Chapter 6

The Imam's Secret Handshake

I was so keen to please the imam that I started rushing to the mosque after school so that he would give me extra jobs. Usually I just cleaned the downstairs toilets – three for boys and three for girls. There was another one upstairs for his personal use but we didn't normally go up there, which is why I was surprised one night when he asked me to clean that one as well.

'Come,' he said, leading me upstairs. 'It's through there.'

Suddenly, I felt nervous. It seemed a bit odd to clean his personal toilet. But then I decided I was being silly. This imam might be horrible to the boys but he'd always been extra nice to me. Now he'd given me even more responsibility and I should feel honoured. I looked down at the toilet bowl. The white porcelain was stained a horrible brownish-gold colour. This was going to need some elbow grease.

'Shall I start?' I asked, looking up at him.

He smiled and cupped my cheek in his hand. I flinched instinctively from his touch, which made him laugh.

'Yes, start in here.'

I scrubbed hard, doing my very best work, until I heard the sound of the children from the mosque bus arriving in the hall below. I used the toilet brush to scrub the last bit of the rim and gave it a final flush. The water cleared, revealing a white, sparkling porcelain bowl beneath.

'Lovely and clean,' I sighed happily, before going to join the other children. A few seemed surprised to see me coming down from upstairs but no one said anything.

The special treatment was making me increasingly unpopular. Two girls who were friends of Farqad's marched up to me in a hostile manner, staring me up and down.

'Look at her,' one said, her voice laced with sarcasm. 'She thinks she's it just because he's picked her. She reckons she's the chosen one.'

'Yeah,' the other girl mimicked. 'Yeah, she thinks she's something special but she's not.'

With that, both girls burst out laughing and walked off.

I looked after them in total bewilderment. I didn't understand what they meant when they said I was the 'chosen one'. It didn't make any sense; all I did was clean for the imam. I was saddened by their attitude. I'd have liked to be friends with these girls but they obviously didn't want me to be.

While I sat cross-legged studying with all the other
children, I mulled over what the girls had said. Why
had he chosen me to clean his toilet and no one else?
Suddenly, out of the blue, I got an overwhelming feeling
that I was being watched. I wondered if it was the nasty
girls and if they were whispering about me. I glanced up
but they were busy reading their prayer books.

My eyes scanned the room. Everyone was sitting in
long lines, reading their prayer books. I let my eyes
roam over the bowed heads until I reached the front of
the room, and that's when I noticed that the imam was
looking directly at me. His stare was intense, as though
he was trying to see right through me. I wondered if he
was just daydreaming. Maybe I only imagined he was
looking at me because his eyes were unfocused. Then,
suddenly, our eyes met and he realised I'd caught him
looking. I drew a deep breath, waiting for him to shout
at me and tell me off for not getting on with my studies,
but instead a sickly smile curled at the corners of his
mouth, revealing his horrible brown teeth.

I couldn't explain it but I felt uneasy. I didn't want
him to notice me and stare at me. I certainly didn't want
him to smile at me. What did he want from me?
Suddenly I was fed up being the special one who cleaned
for him. I wished I could be treated just like all the other
children. I wanted to fade into the background.
Something was wrong, but I couldn't put my finger on
it.

I pulled Mum's scarf tighter around my face and bent
my head to my prayer book. I tried to focus on the
words written on the pages but I was so nervous that I

couldn't make them out. They blurred and danced in a jumbled mess until they were just lines and squiggles. I rubbed at my eyes.

Farqad sensed that something was wrong and turned to me. 'What's the matter?' she asked.

'Nothing,' I whispered as I looked back at the book. I prayed that the imam wouldn't pick me to go out and read for him that night. He would often pick a child to go and read for him at the front of the room. If you got it right you could return to your seat, but if you got it wrong you'd be punished with a push or a slap as an example to the others. Farqad told me he even slapped the girls, which was unheard of. They weren't beaten as hard as the boys, but if they were caught chatting the imam would think nothing of hitting them across the hand. I'd not witnessed it myself – I must have been upstairs cleaning for him at the time – but it seems the girls concerned were too terrified to tell their parents. If they were anything like mine, their mums and dads would probably turn a blind eye anyway.

I became scared of being called up to read, especially now that he had begun to stare at me in such an odd way. I heard him call a name and at first I couldn't make it out. I took a deep breath. When I realised it wasn't mine, I slowly let the air escape from my lungs. I was safe for another day at least.

Around this time, I started to look upon the imam differently and I saw how he loved the power he had, strutting around the hall like a peacock, pulling at his sarong and barking out orders. He believed that he was the most important man in our lives – and in many

ways he was. He commanded respect, and if you didn't
show it you'd be punished. Here in the mosque he was
the judge and the jury and he administered the punish-
ments as well.

In many ways, I felt grateful for my chores because
they spared me from the risk of incurring a punishment.
There was so much to wash, clean and tidy that sometimes he called me out in the middle of lessons. At least
when I was cleaning I was safe – out of sight and out of
mind. When I cleaned his kitchen or toilet upstairs, I
was away from his staring eyes because he had to stay
downstairs to look after his students.

Eventually, he asked some of the other girls to help
me in the kitchen, and I felt relieved. Maybe they'd stop
being mean to me now. However, the imam said I was
the only one allowed to clean his personal toilet. I
convinced myself that it didn't mean anything. It was
only a stupid toilet and he'd ask someone else to take
their turn before long. But weeks passed, and that
stinky toilet remained my responsibility and no one
else's.

One evening, I arrived at the mosque and walked
over to the imam to shake his hand as usual. As I
approached him, his eyes flashed with a look of something – was it recognition? I couldn't be sure. I held out
my hand and he grabbed it, looking me directly in the
eye. I wanted to look away but I was too frightened. A
cold chill ran through my body. I didn't understand
why I felt so uneasy. Maybe it was because of the
strange smile playing at the corners of his mouth.
Maybe it was the fact that he held onto my hand for

longer than usual, as if he didn't want to let it go. Nothing was said after the normal greetings, but still he held my hand.

When he let go, I shook the uneasiness from my mind, collected my prayer book and waited for the others to arrive. The imam watched me as I went to take my place. Soon the other children had filled the mosque. As usual, they burst in through the doors *en masse*. Farqad came in and smiled, gesturing at me to save a space for her, and I nodded back. Moments later she was at my side, but I still felt self-conscious because the imam was looking over. I grabbed Mum's headscarf and pulled it tighter around my head so that it almost swamped my face. I wanted to hide behind it. I wanted to disappear.

Farqad turned to me. I was trying to act normal, but I didn't feel it.

'What's up? You look upset,' she said, her voice full of concern.

'No,' I replied, 'I'm fine.'

The scarf became my mask. I used it to cover my face as much as I could to stop the imam from looking at me. Something was wrong. I could feel it. I didn't understand why he kept looking at me in such a peculiar way and it made me cross and upset and disturbed. The more I thought about it, the more I fretted. I wondered if I'd done something wrong. Without realising what I was doing, I pulled at the edge of the scarf and began to grind it between my back teeth. By the end of the lesson I'd sucked and chewed on it so hard that I'd bitten a hole right through it. As I poked my fingertip through the fabric, I suddenly panicked. What would Mum say? She'd go mad.

Mum got furious when I didn't take care of my clothes. She often caught me scraping my ugly brown school shoes along the pavement, hoping in vain to destroy them. I wished I could have pretty, shiny black shoes like the other girls at school, but Mum had bought me an ugly yet indestructible brown pair.

'Tough!' she said, slapping the backs of my legs. 'I know what you're trying to do and it won't work. I've paid good money for those shoes and they are going to last you.'

When I rolled around the floor in play rough-and-tumble with my brothers and Dad, she would grumble under her breath that I would tear my blouse or trousers and she would have to be the one to mend them.

So I knew I'd be in hot water if she noticed that I'd bitten a hole right through her headscarf.

Farqad saw the hole and clasped her hand to her mouth in horror, saying 'Uh-oh!', which made me feel even worse.

As I left the mosque that night, I folded the scarf neatly several times over, being careful to hide the hole beneath layers of fabric, and I pushed it deep down inside the lining of my coat pocket where it could remain hidden from my mother.

The following evening I hung around after tea, reluctant to go to the mosque early.

'What are you doing? Off you go. Get out from under my feet,' Mum ordered in Urdu, so I had no choice but to pull on my coat and leave, although the time was only twenty-five past four on the kitchen clock.

I dawdled, dragging my feet on the way down the busy main road, but there was only so long I could make the journey take. I thought about hanging around on the corner outside to wait for the mosque bus, but if someone who knew me drove past they'd be sure to tell my parents. Standing on street corners wasn't something a good Muslim girl should be seen doing. I couldn't win. I had to go inside.

I tried to sneak in through the door, shutting it quietly so that it wouldn't bang. As I knelt to remove my shoes, I watched the carpet in front of me and suddenly two filthy feet appeared, with long, curved toenails like claws. My heart sank. It was the imam, waiting for me. I was the only one there again. I glanced nervously at the clock on the wall: quarter to five. The other children would be on the bus by now and they'd be here in less than fifteen minutes. I wanted to go straight to the bench to get away from the imam but I couldn't be rude.

I held out my hand to shake his. He grabbed it, smiling. I lowered my gaze, my palm clammy with sweat and nerves, and repeated the greeting. This time, instead of replying as he should have done, the imam stroked the inside of my palm with his index finger. I was puzzled. Was he trying to tickle me? Was it a joke? Did he want me to do it back to him?

He pushed his index finger hard into the palm of my hand as if to make a point. It felt uncomfortable and silly at the same time. Was it some kind of special ritual I hadn't yet been taught?

Finally, he spoke – 'Alaikum salaam' – and chuckled, as if we had shared a joke between us.

When he let go of my hand, I walked warily across the room to the bench and stood on top of it to reach for my prayer book. I sat down, keeping my back flat against the wall, with one eye on the imam and the other on the clock that hung high on the opposite wall. The red hand moved round slowly, ticking off each and every second. The imam was standing by the door but he was still watching me. Why was he watching me?

'The children will be here soon,' I told myself.

I opened my prayer book and pretended to read but in my head I was counting the seconds until the others would arrive. I didn't have to look up to know that he was still watching me, but nothing was said. The silence felt awkward and uncomfortable. I could hear myself breathing and tried to make my breath quieter. I shrank back against the wall to try and make myself smaller, but all the time I could feel those eyes upon me.

At last, I heard the excited chatter of children's voices filling the air as they streamed off the bus. The door burst open, and finally they were there. Within minutes dozens of kids had descended on the mosque like a horde of locusts. Each one queued up to take turns shaking the imam's hand. I watched each handshake carefully. It was hard to tell from where I was sitting but I didn't think he was doing that tickling finger thing with anyone else. All the other handshakes looked normal. None of them took more than a couple of seconds.

Then it struck me: that handshake had been especially for me and now it now hung in the air between us, like a secret.

Those girls had been right. I must be the chosen one.

Chapter 7

The Chosen One

A week after the incident with the funny handshake, when I once again arrived at the mosque early despite my best efforts to delay the journey, the imam called down the stairs to me. 'You might as well come and sit up in my office to learn your prayers, rather than being down there all on your own.'

'OK,' I replied. He hadn't done anything weird since the handshake and I'd convinced myself it had just been a joke. He'd even stopped looking at me the whole time, which was a huge relief. I needed to stop over-reacting and worrying so much.

As I walked into the imam's office, he was sitting at a big mahogany table in the centre of the room. The office was large and dark. Heavy red velvet curtains were pulled tightly shut against the front windows so the only light was a yellowish glow coming from a single lightbulb, which hung from the middle of the ceiling. There were books lying around on the table and floor. Then I glanced down at the other end of the room and was shocked to notice a big double bed in the corner. I'd never been in a man's bedroom before, but here I was, in the imam's bedroom. I knew it was forbidden. I shouldn't be in any man's bedroom, least of all the imam's. He seemed to live by a different set of rules than the ones I'd been brought up with, and it made me feel very uncertain.

Although the room was large it felt cramped with the big wooden table, the bed, the books and the general mess all over the floor. There were clothes strewn around the bed, as though he'd just simply thrown them off at night without a care where they landed.

The imam pulled a book towards him, opened the cover and flicked quickly through the pages.

'You can learn your prayers early, before the others get here, then you'll be done,' he suggested. 'That way, you'll have plenty of time to do the cleaning.'

It made sense, I supposed. I glanced at some of the other books on the table. The imam noticed me turning my head to try and read the upside-down covers and he pushed a pile of books over towards me.

'Look at them if you want,' he offered.

As I started to flick through a few, he busied himself with the Koran. A moment later he had another suggestion.

'It would be useful if you could do a bit of tidying in here as well as the kitchen and bathroom.'

I glanced across the room at the unmade bed and messy clothes and didn't know what to say. Was I meant to tidy *them*?

'OK,' I replied weakly.

The teacher smiled warmly and patted me on the head, then his hand stroked down the side of my head, where he could feel one of my plaits coiled under my headscarf.

'Such a beautiful girl,' he said wistfully. 'We'll read together first and then you can tidy.' He pulled the book closer in front of him.

I was standing by the side of the table, a few feet away.

'You can't see from over there, Nabila. Come closer.'

I nodded but it felt strange. No one else was here, only us, and I didn't know what I was expected to do. But he was the imam, I told myself – my teacher. I had to do as he asked, so I stepped around the desk, positioned myself by his side and began to read.

'Good, good, you are learning fast,' he nodded approvingly as I finished a prayer.

His praise made me feel good. He must like me a lot. He must think I was a really good student.

'One of my daughters is about your age,' he said. 'I miss them very much.'

'How old is your other daughter?' I asked.

The imam got up and crossed the room to a chest of drawers on the side. He opened the top drawer and pulled out a photograph, then laid it on the table and pointed at the two little girls in the picture. There was the one my age, and another who looked about two years old. The imam studied the photograph and sighed to himself.

'My daughter is clever and pretty, just like you. I love my family very much, and I miss them. I miss Bangladesh. But I couldn't pass up this opportunity to teach at a mosque in England. It is a big honour for me. Still, it is hard to be away from my wife. She writes to me every week with the news from back home, and I keep all her letters.'

I felt sorry for him, imagining how homesick he must feel. He was a proud father, just like my own dad. Even though he was the imam, he was still a normal human being.

'You have finished your prayers, so you can tidy up in here now,' he said, putting the photograph back in the drawer. 'You could start by sorting through my books. That would be a big help, but you mustn't move any of the papers on my desk.'

He sat down at the desk again and I started to sort through the dusty old prayer books on the side. No wonder he didn't want anyone else up here because it was filthy, even worse than the kitchen! The room had a horrible rancid stench of body odour and festering socks. I hadn't noticed it when I was busy trying to read my prayers, but the more I moved around the room the more I could smell it. I tried not to breathe in too deeply.

I wondered why he kept the windows shut. If he opened them it would let out the smell of sweaty feet and stinky armpits. Surely it must bother him as well as me? Or had he become immune to it?

It wasn't just the smell that bothered me, but the clutter and mess. Back home our new house was always neat and tidy – Mum insisted upon it. Even my lazy brothers had to put their own stuff away. But this room looked more like a jumble sale, with clothes strewn everywhere. A huge pile had been dumped in the middle of the floor and I was grateful that it wasn't my job to clear them.

The imam asked me to arrange all the books in the bookcase. I worked carefully, placing each book in order of size, starting with the smallest on the left and continuing along to the larger ones on the right. As I shuffled them around I sneaked a peak behind me at the big double bed in the corner of the room. It had a red velvet throw across it, the same colour as the curtains, but the covers were rumpled up and a couple of pillows were propped up against the headboard. Even at that distance I could see the pillowcases were stained a yellowish-brown colour where his body had leant up against them. I wondered how long it had been since he'd changed his bed linen. I'd never seen anyone live in such squalor before. No wonder he missed his wife! He needed someone to do his laundry and clean his rooms for him because he obviously wasn't managing on his own.

A red patterned carpet ran across the room, covering the entire length, but it was so grubby that it was hard to make out the original pattern. I began to pick up some books and papers that had been dropped on the floor and then I saw something that made me blush – a pair of stained black underpants. They must be the imam's because they were the same kind he wore when he knelt down in front of us in the mosque. They made me want to gag. My face felt hot and I flushed with embarrassment. I'd had to put my brothers' underpants in the washing machine before, but I'd never seen anything like this – dirty pants in the middle of the floor. I thought how horrified Mum would be.

This imam was as scruffy and dirty as a tramp. I wondered what the other kids would think if they were standing where I was standing right now.

Soon, the sound of children's voices filled the hall below. I glanced towards the door.

'Everybody's coming,' the imam said, jumping to his feet. 'We'd better go downstairs.'

The children were still flooding in through the mosque door in such a rush that no one noticed the imam and me coming downstairs together. They were all too busy taking off their shoes and chatting to those beside them. I wandered over to my usual place next to Farqad and the lesson began.

I didn't tell my best friend I'd been in the imam's bedroom because I wasn't sure if I should. She might tell the others and if word got back to the imam he would be angry with me for telling.

That night the imam talked to us about the customary greeting and handshake we should give whenever we meet another Muslim person. Soon the children were giggling as they practised both the greeting and the handshake with each other. I thought about the imam's special handshake with the wiggling finger and wondered yet again what it meant. None of the other children were doing it that way. Thinking about it made me shiver.

It seemed that a precedent had been set that night, because the next time I arrived at the mosque early the

imam once again called me upstairs to the office to read
my prayers to him.

I stood next to him, but instead of looking at the
book he looked directly at me.

'Aren't you a pretty girl?' he whispered in my ear.

I wasn't sure if it was a question or a compliment.
What should I say in reply? I tried to move a little
further away from him because I could smell his stinky
breath, with the rotten old food smell, and it made me
want to retch. He was staring at me again and that
made me very uncomfortable, so I tried to focus all my
attention on the book that was open in front of us and
I willed him to look at it too.

'You've got such lovely hair, Nabila,' he sighed, and
he slipped his hand underneath my headscarf to touch
it. I jerked back instinctively but he kept his hand there,
stroking my plaits.

'And your eyes are so big and beautiful,' he continued, gazing at me.

I liked it when he gave me special tasks to do, I liked
it when he let me off with my prayers, but I didn't like
this. I wanted him to stop looking at me, to stop touching my hair and to stop saying these strange things. My
mum always told me I was pretty, but that was different
– she was my mum. This was the imam, the leader of
the community, and it felt all wrong for him to be telling me he liked my hair and my eyes.

He slid his hand out from under the scarf and I
breathed a sigh of relief. That was it; it was over. But
then he stretched out a single finger. I saw it out of the
corner of my eye. It hovered towards my face, then he

ran the edge of his finger down my cheek. My skin
crawled at his touch. He was a man, like my dad – but
he wasn't like my dad at all. My dad was touchy-feely
and would always give me lots of hugs and kisses, but
not like this. He wouldn't stroke my face. I didn't like it
at all.

The mosque door crashed open and the sound of
children's voices drifted upstairs.

Without another word the imam rose to his feet and
walked off, leaving me alone. I felt scared and confused.
Did he want me to clean again? I supposed he must, so
I picked up a cloth and gave his office a quick dust.
Once I had finished, I slipped downstairs to join the
others.

Children were still queuing, waiting to shake his
hand, so I joined the end of the queue. My heart beat
louder and louder as I got near the imam. Soon, I stood
before him and he held out his hand. He grasped my
hand and I wanted to die of embarrassment when I felt
his finger in my palm and realised he was doing that
funny handshake again. My eyes darted around me to
see if anyone had noticed. There were kids everywhere.
I glanced up at him, pleading with my eyes for him to
stop. It wasn't funny any more. The imam had a strange
smile on his face, as if it were a joke, but he didn't
laugh. I got the feeling he was amused by my reaction.

He let go of my hand and beckoned the next child
forward. I watched carefully as he shook that boy's
hand but there was no wiggling finger – just a handshake. I waited for a girl to reach the top of the queue
and watched again, to see if he maybe only did it with

girls, but he just gave her a normal handshake. It looked as though the secret kind were just for me. I hated it, and wished he wouldn't do it. I wished he wouldn't stroke my hair and tell me I was pretty. I hated the way he had touched my cheek.

Maybe in Bangladesh these things were perfectly normal, but here I knew they were peculiar and wrong and I'd have given anything for him to treat me exactly the same as the other children. I didn't want to be his chosen one any more.

Chapter 8

Secret Lessons

I didn't have to go to the mosque at weekends so I spent the time doing my homework and helping Mum around the house. I tried to keep busy but Mum noticed there was something on my mind.

'What's the matter with you?' she asked, as we made the beds together.

My heart thumped. I wondered if she somehow knew about the imam and his special handshake.

'Nothing,' I lied. 'Why?'

'It's just that you're normally such a chatterbox but today you seem … I don't know … you seem quieter than usual.' She tucked a sheet neatly under one of the corners of the bed.

I shrugged, but Mum wasn't letting it go.

'You're not sickening for something, are you?' She walked over and placed a cool hand on my forehead.

'You feel warm but you don't feel hot. If you're not well, you'll tell me, won't you?'

'Yes,' I replied.

I wanted to tell my mother all about the imam's funny handshake and his stroking my hair and my cheek and how it made me feel, but I thought she would be cross with me. I'd heard her telling Dad that everyone said the new imam was brilliant and how great it was that they had someone in the post who would stay there long-term now. If I said anything bad about him, first of all she wouldn't believe me, and second, she would be furious with me for speaking against a holy man. Everyone in the family accused me of being a scaredy-cat after the incident of the fox that I thought was a wolf. I was the baby of the family, the girly girl, and, as such, not to be taken seriously.

No, I thought to myself. It'd be best to keep quiet. Habib was right. I just had to do what the imam said and then he wouldn't get angry. Anyway, he'd soon get tired of me when he realised how useless I was at the Koran. He'd pick out another girl to do the special tasks and I'd be forgotten.

The following week the imam didn't invite me upstairs. When I arrived at the mosque early he left me on my own downstairs to read my prayer book. What did it mean? Had I angered or upset him in some way? I was disconcerted but at the same time relieved. Maybe my spell of being the special one was over and he would treat me just the same as everyone else from now on.

But I'd got my hopes up prematurely. It wasn't long before he called me up to the office once more, and this time I crept up the stairs, wide-eyed and apprehensive. Was he going to stroke my hair or touch my cheek? How could I stop him? By the time I reached his office he already had the prayer book open in front of him on the desk.

'Come closer, let's say your prayers,' he urged.

I stood at the corner of the desk and began to read, but he pulled the book further away from me so that I couldn't see it clearly any more.

'No, no,' he tutted, 'you can't see from over there. Come here,' he said, patting his hand against his bare thigh.

I was horrified. There was no way I was going to sit on his lap. No way.

He sensed my shock and laughed. He pushed the book even further away from me. I craned my head to try and read the words, but it was impossible. I had to move closer to him so that I could see. I wondered if it was some kind of game.

'Closer, Nabila,' he whispered, shifting the book away from me a third time. I took another sideways step. By now we were almost touching. When he exhaled, his stinky breath felt hot against my neck.

But I couldn't disobey the imam. I had to do as he said. If I didn't, he might slap me the way he slapped the other girls. He might even beat me with a stick, as he'd done to that boy. I didn't dare say no. By now we were so close that I could feel the heat of his skin against mine. Suddenly, he looped his arm around my waist and pulled me even closer. My body stiffened.

'There,' he said. 'That's better, isn't it?'

But it wasn't. It wasn't better for me. It felt wrong. The imam kept his hand hooked around my waist and I could feel the heat of his palm through my thin cotton top. It felt clammy, like a leech that was stuck to me. I wanted to rip it off and run away, but I wasn't brave enough.

'Now let's begin,' he said, tapping a dirty finger against the page of the open book.

'*Read, Nabila, just read*,' I told myself. '*The quicker you read, the quicker you can get away*.' Only I couldn't. I tried to say the words but my voice was barely a whisper. A hard lump was lodged high up in my windpipe. I could barely breathe, never mind talk.

I wriggled about in his grasp, trying to get away from him, but the more I moved the tighter he held on. Now I was stuck, rooted to the spot. There was no escape, not until the children arrived downstairs. Only their presence could save me now.

As soon as the bus pulled up and we could hear the children coming into the hall, the imam let go. My legs felt unsteady as I dashed downstairs to join them. He wasn't supposed to do things like that – it was all wrong. I'd never been held by another man like that. When our old nosey neighbour Aariz came to the house we shook hands and said the formal greeting, but he wouldn't dream of putting an arm round my waist. My brothers wouldn't even do that to me. I *knew* it shouldn't be happening.

I found it hard to focus for the rest of the evening. Farqad thought I was being off with her but my mind was whirring with everything that had happened in his office. It wasn't right. He was my teacher and he wasn't supposed to behave that way. I wondered if it had been some sort of trial or game, a challenge that I had to pass – but for what purpose? The thought stayed in my head long after I'd climbed into bed that night, where I fell into a fitful sleep.

The following morning I woke up and felt something cold and wet against my legs. I threw back the covers and gasped in horror when I saw there was a big golden-yellow circle right underneath my bum. I'd wet the bed. I was almost eight years old, yet I'd wet myself. I hadn't done that since I was a baby. I was disgusted and ashamed.

I pulled off my sodden pyjamas as fast as I could. Wee had soaked all along the back of them and down the legs. I'd also managed to wet the hem of my pyjama top. I had to hide the damp clothes quickly, before Mum found them. She'd go mad. I rolled them up and stuffed them down the side of the bed, then stepped back to check they couldn't be seen. I couldn't decide what to do with the wet sheet, though. I fretted and couldn't seem to think straight. Finally I came up with a plan. If I flipped the mattress over so the wet patch faced downwards and turned the sheet around the other way, I could sleep on the still-dry half of the sheet that night. The wet side would be tucked down at the bottom of the bed, out of sight.

When I'd finished, everything looked normal but it also looked too neat. Mum might have been suspicious, so I ruffled the top covers to make it a little messy.

By this stage I was running late for school and had no time for a wash. I opened my drawer and pulled on a fresh pair of pants. My school had just introduced a uniform but it wasn't compulsory. I'd begged Mum to buy me the grey trousers and blue jumper because I thought they made me look and feel grown-up – but I felt far from that right now, after wetting the bed like a baby. I still felt ashamed as I groped under the bed, searching for my school shoes, and smelled the tell-tale scent of urine on the mattress.

I twirled around, looking at myself in my dressing table mirror from every angle. I appeared the same, but something had changed. I felt different. I lifted my arm and had a quick sniff at my jumper. It smelled fresh but I knew the truth – that underneath my clothes my body was dirty and smelled of wee. I fretted that the other children would smell it on me at school. They'd tease me and I'd lose all my friends, which would be awful. No one would want to be friends with a girl who wet the bed. I was dirty, just like the imam.

I opened my bedroom door and did one last scan of the room before I shut it and went downstairs to breakfast.

Thankfully, no one noticed the smell of wee at school that day. I ran around madly in the playground hoping that the fresh air would blow me clean.

That night, as soon as I got home from school, I changed out of my uniform and pulled on fresh pants, a top and trousers. I checked the bed again before I left for the mosque, and it looked normal. The wet circle on the sheet had dried to a pale golden ring, which was

barely visible. I'd got away with it. Mum did the washing every weekend, so I'd just have to use the same sheet
until then, when I'd be able to sneak it into the washing
machine with my pyjamas and the other laundry.

By the time I got to the mosque, I was still so worried
about wetting myself that at first I didn't notice the
imam standing there. He beckoned me over and indicated that I was to come upstairs with him. I took each
step slowly, like a condemned man on his way to the
noose.

Once we were in his room he sat down at the desk,
grabbed at my waist greedily and pulled me to him. No
more fun and games – he was in charge, and I was his
possession now. I tried to ignore his hand resting heavily on my hip. Instead, I cleared my throat and began to
read.

'*Just pretend you're somewhere else, Nabila, then
everything will be all right,*' I told myself. '*Don't make
him angry.*'

The imam slipped his arm from around from my
waist and began to rub the centre of my back. His hand
moved rhythmically up my spine and down to the base
of my bum. I flinched and waited for an apology. Surely
it must have been accidental when he touched my bum?
He carried on rubbing, though, as if there was nothing
to worry about, until eventually I finished my prayers.

'Tidy my books, but not the ones that are open,' he
said gruffly. 'If they're open it's because I'm still reading
them, or doing some work from them.'

'OK,' I replied in a whisper. I was just glad to be out
of his arms.

I spent the next ten minutes clearing the books but all the time I kept an eye on the imam, where he sat reading quietly at his desk, in case he decided to make a grab for me again.

As soon as I heard the other children arrive I bolted over towards the door. This was my cue to go downstairs. No one noticed as I crept into the mosque and blended silently into the crowd. No one noticed the imam following me. No one noticed that I was pale and silent with shock about what had occurred. Even Farqad didn't notice anything unusual, and I certainly didn't tell her what had happened. I couldn't tell anyone. It was too awful.

That evening, during lessons, the imam called out my name. My heart froze but he just wanted me to clean the toilet upstairs, so I shot straight to my feet. I was happy to do it because it meant I didn't have to be in the same room as him.

'Can Farqad help me, please?' I stuttered nervously.

Her eyes lit up and she nodded eagerly. She'd never been in his private rooms before and she wanted to have a look.

'No, just you,' the imam said coldly. 'She's got to practise her prayers.'

Farqad looked crushed. She'd been shown up in front of all the others.

'You're cleverer than them, Nabila,' the imam continued, gesturing at the other children in the hall. 'You know your prayers already, and that's why you are allowed to go up and clean for me.'

Farqad and the others looked at me in astonishment. It was quite clearly a lie. I was the slowest learner of the whole group and they all knew it. I hated learning the Koran – I found it difficult and I was nowhere near the top of the class. Farqad was much better than me. She was the best of all of us.

I wondered what she would say if I told her the real reason the imam had chosen me was because he wanted to wrap his arms around me, rub my back and stroke my cheeks. I was sure she wouldn't believe me. No one would.

As I climbed the stairs I looked forlornly back at my friends seated in the hall below. I'd been separated from them again. I was worried that they'd imagine I thought I was better than them. In truth, I never thought that. I was Nabila, the girl who was rubbish at the Koran and rubbish at lessons – I had no interest in them at all. But I was good at one thing; I was good at being pretty. I had a bum, little boobs and curvy hips and the imam had taken a shine to me. I didn't want to be Nabila any more. I wanted to go back to being a little girl who sat chatting with her friends.

Later that night, as I pulled on my shoes, a few girls came over to taunt me.

'Look at her! She thinks she's a princess or something. It's not fair that she doesn't have to learn her prayers!'

I looked to Farqad for support but she just bowed her head and concentrated on her shoelaces. I was all on my own.

'I'm sorry, I asked if you could help but he wouldn't let me,' I told Farqad.

'It doesn't matter,' she shrugged, but I could tell that it did.

'Look,' I said, wrapping my arm around her shoulder. 'You're far cleverer than me and that's why I need you. You have to help me to learn so that I can get out of here. I hate it!'

'But I thought you were the clever one,' she said sarcastically. 'Why does he ask you to clean all the time if you're not clever?'

'Because I'm a bit thick,' I replied, trying to turn the tables on myself. 'He probably thinks I'm only good for cleaning poo from his mucky, horrible, stinky toilet!'

Farqad thought for a moment and laughed.

'Okay,' she said. 'Of course I'll help you. The sooner we can all get out of this place, the better.'

Chapter 9

The Imam's Bite

My lovely friend Farqad began to help me recite passages from the Koran every night we were at the mosque, listening patiently and correcting me.

'No, Nabila, you've missed out that bit,' she said, pointing to some words on the page.

I huffed sadly. I seemed to have a mental block for some of the weird Urdu phrases and could never get them right.

'Sorry,' I said, and tried again, over and over, until I'd memorised it perfectly.

'Good,' she commented. 'At least the imam won't shout at you now.'

I caught her gaze and we both looked down, slightly embarrassed. I felt my face flush because we both knew the imam never shouted at me, only at the other children.

With Farqad helping me, I hoped that it wouldn't be long before I finished my time at the mosque. My eighth birthday came and went and I focused as hard as I could on my studies, but the imam's strange behaviour was never far from my thoughts.

A few weeks after the back-stroking incident I was reading to him in his room when I felt a hand on my thigh. I gasped with fright, stopped reading and turned towards him. He didn't move.

'Continue,' he insisted, pointing at the book with his left hand.

I tried to read some more but then he moved his right hand along the top of my thigh, over my trousers. Every time his hand rose higher, I flinched. I was terrified because I didn't know why he was doing this. I was too frightened to tell him off or say no. My whole body started to tremble and I stared blankly at the open page in front of me. The words were dancing around on the page as I tried to focus.

'If you don't read, then you won't learn,' the imam scolded.

I wanted to finish my reading. I wanted the other children to arrive, and for me to be back downstairs and away from the imam's smelly office-cum-bedroom so I continued to read. But then he moved his hand from the front of my thigh and around to my bum. He began to caress and stroke it over the top of my clothes. I didn't know what to do. This felt really wrong – I knew for sure it was wrong – but I was confused because I still had my clothes on. I wondered if this is what he did to his own daughters in Bangladesh. I wondered if this was considered normal out there. But he was the imam, the one who was supposed to judge right from wrong. That's what he was here to teach me.

'You are such a pretty girl,' he whispered, his breath hot against my neck. 'So beautiful.'

His voice trailed off as he leaned in to kiss my cheek. I steeled myself. It felt creepy and disgusting. He wasn't my boyfriend, but here he was kissing me as if I was a girlfriend, someone he loved. My heart was beating hard, like a wild animal in a cage, as his hot rubbery lips rubbed against my cheeks. Every instinct told me to run away from him but I couldn't because panic had rooted me to the spot.

The following evening, the same thing happened but this time the imam kissed my face in an urgent and more frenzied way. I shut my eyes and screwed up my nose. I could feel his hot, wet tongue licking at the side of my face. His hairy beard scratched and tickled my skin and I could smell the dirty straggly hair. I wanted to throw up right there and then. I wanted to push him away. His tongue made a horrible slurping sound. I tried to block him out. I tried to imagine that I was having my face licked by a cute little puppy, but it was no good.

I knew this was very wrong. Every muscle in my body went rigid. I wanted him to stop but he wouldn't. I knew he shouldn't be doing this to me. I was a child, yet he kissed me the way I'd seen adults kissing in films on the telly. You weren't supposed to kiss children like that, but now the imam was doing it to me and I was too frightened to say no. He was in charge; he was the teacher.

I tried pulling away from him but he just pulled me back again. The more I struggled, the more he laughed, as if we were playing a silly game. This was a game – his game – but it wasn't any fun. It was an uneven struggle in which he was the cat and I was the little mouse.

His stinking breath engulfed the side of my neck and face. I tried not to breathe because I didn't want to inhale his breath down into my own lungs. I didn't want him to become part of me.

'You are so very beautiful,' he said, cupping my cheeks.

People said it all the time as they squeezed my cheeks. My parent's friends said it, Mum said it and so did Dad, but this was different. As the imam squeezed my cheeks hard between his bony fingertips I winced in pain. This wasn't someone being nice – this was horrible and frightening.

Afterwards I felt numb, like a person in a trance. As we walked home Habib commented on how quiet I was, but he was the last person I could talk to about it. As soon as we got back I went into the kitchen where Mum was cooking dinner for Dad and stood watching her, trying to think how I could tell her what had happened, feeling safe just being in her presence.

'I hate going to the mosque, Mum,' I whispered.

'Too bad. You're going anyway. We've had this discussion before.'

'I can't bear it,' I said, trying to make my voice sound desperate.

'Why are you always the drama queen? And you have to choose the moments when I am busiest. Go and talk to your brothers, Nabila. I've had enough of you for today.'

I slunk out of the kitchen and up to my bedroom. There was no way I could talk to my brothers about this. They'd tell me I was a liar and a fantasist, then they'd make fun of me. I could just imagine Habib saying, 'Nabila thinks the imam is in love with her. What an idiot. Who could ever be in love with someone as silly as her?'

I had no one to turn to. No one would believe me when it was my word against that of an imam. My next plan was to try and reduce the time I had on my own with him by making myself arrive later. I'd hang around at home until Mum had to shoo me out the door, then I'd walk down the road as slowly as it was humanly possible to do. Once I tried walking round the block to waste time but a neighbour saw me and asked what I was doing.

'Aren't you on your way to the mosque, Nabila? Hurry up. You don't want to be late now.'

Even when I thought I'd been particularly slow, I'd arrive at the mosque to find there were still ten minutes left before the bus was due to arrive and the imam would be standing on the stairs, beckoning me upwards. Either that, or he'd lead me upstairs after the last child had disappeared, knowing there would be as much as half an hour to spare before Habib arrived to pick me up.

When he heard my brother at the door, the imam would hurry down to say hello. Sometimes he had an official letter of some kind that he asked Habib to translate into Urdu because his English wasn't very good. He couldn't understand letters from the tax office or the council or the department of immigration, but Habib was always happy to explain what they said, while I stood flushed and hot with shame about what the imam had been doing to me upstairs only moments before.

The licking and sucking continued for months and months. I would hear his gulps by my ear and the smacking sound of his wet lips against my flesh. Then one day his teeth closed on the flesh of my cheek and he began to suck. It was painful with his mouth clamped against me, and when the pain got too much I let out a yelp. He released me but then he bit me again, as if he couldn't resist.

I looked at him resentfully, my eyes full of tears. He'd bitten me like an animal. I could still feel my cheek throbbing. I had no idea why he would do something like that. Kissing me was one thing, but biting was something else entirely.

I expected him to apologise, as if this was a game that had gone too far. A silence hung between us but he wouldn't look at me. Instead he looked back down at the book on the desk.

'You have finished here, so go downstairs now,' he said at last, turning away from me as if I was the one who'd done something wrong.

I dashed for the door and ran downstairs, straight to one of the girls' toilets. Pushing the door closed, I bolted it shut. I rested my back against the cool wooden surface and allowed myself to slide down into a heap on the floor. My throat had become tight with fear. It felt all closed up and I was struggling to breathe. My hands trembled and my heart was pounding beneath my ribcage.

The imam had bitten me. I shook my head in disbelief. Why would he do that? Maybe I'd been naughty and this was my punishment, but I couldn't imagine what I'd done wrong. I always did my best to please him. Hot tears rolled down my cheeks, stinging the sore place where he'd bitten me. My legs were like jelly and I felt as if I'd never be able to stand again. My whole body shook. What he'd done was wrong. It wasn't nice. There was no way imams were supposed to behave like this. He was banking on me not telling anyone. Perhaps he sensed that I was too much of a coward to stand up to him. That's why he'd picked me – because I'd be too scared to tell. I shivered, feeling freezing cold even though it was warm in the mosque. I think I was in shock.

After a few deep breaths, I managed to pull myself to my feet. My legs felt unsteady, as if they might give way at any moment. I staggered over to the small sink that was attached to the wall, turned the cold tap on full and pushed the black rubber plug in the centre. Icy water gushed in. Scooping my hands, I splashed water on my face. It was so cold that for a moment it stole my breath away again.

The children would be here soon. I had to get myself clean. I had to look normal.

I grasped the grey-white bar of soap between my hands. It was soggy and squirmed beneath my fingers.

I rubbed the soap against my palms but it was cheap and hard to lather. I rubbed my hands against my face and neck and splashed myself with water once more, then pulled a green paper towel from the holder. It felt rough against my face but I rubbed and rubbed, desperate to remove every last bit of the imam's spit. The thought of his stinking gob on my cheek made my flesh crawl.

I smoothed my hair and washed my hands twice more. The soap left them dry but at least now they were squeaky clean.

Soon the sound of excited chatter filled the room next door. The other children were here. I wasn't alone any more.

Sliding the bolt aside, I opened the door and stepped out of the toilet, trying to look normal. As I walked over to get my prayer book, I spotted Farqad taking off her shoes by the door. I waved and she waved back, then moments later she was by my side.

'Hi,' she said breezily as she sat down on the floor next to me.

I flashed her my brightest smile as if everything was okay, but her expression turned to one of horror.

'What's happened to your face?' she gasped.

I lifted my fingers to the spot where the imam had bitten my cheek.

'Er … what?' I asked, pretending I didn't have a clue what she was talking about.

'Your face, Nabila. It looks all red and sore.' She touched it gently with her fingertip, peering at the wound closely. 'Has someone hit you? It wasn't one of your brothers, was it?' Her voice became stern. 'I bet it was Tariq.'

'No, no!' I protested. I looked at her for a moment and wished I could tell her the truth, but it was too big a truth. I turned away, and shook my head. 'Silly me! I sat too close to the fire, that's all.' The lie came into my head because I was often accused of doing this back home.

Farqad narrowed her eyes. I could tell she didn't believe me. 'It doesn't look like a burn to me. If it was one of your brothers, you would tell me, wouldn't you?'

I had to convince her. 'Of course I would, but it wasn't them – honest! It was the fire. I just sat too close to it when Mum was doing my hair. She's always telling me off about it. Anyway,' I sighed, opening up my prayer book, 'let's start. What does this word mean? I've never come across it before. I can't even pronounce it.'

Farqad glanced at my book and told me the word. I'd convinced her for now. If only I could have confided in her. She knew what the imam was like, with his black underpants and his smelly breath. She knew that he often made me clean the rooms upstairs, giving us ample time alone together. She would surely believe me, even if no one else did. But I couldn't bear to tell her. I couldn't bear it if she thought I was making it up to seem special. I couldn't bear it if she *did* believe me but thought it was somehow my own fault. And so I didn't tell her the truth, and the moment had passed.

At the end of the lesson I had to wait for Habib, and I was terrified that the imam would try to bite me again.

I'd never felt so alone and vulnerable. He didn't try anything else that night, though, just reading his books while I waited downstairs, watching the clock and the mosque door.

As soon as Habib arrived I ran over to him. He called up to the imam to say goodnight and the imam shouted back down.

'Let's get going,' I whispered, tugging his arm.

'Hey, what's the rush?' Habib asked as I fled through the mosque door onto the street outside.

'I just want to get home. I'm tired,' I lied. That was two lies – to Farqad and now Habib. I was getting good at them.

I went straight up to my bedroom that night saying I didn't want any dinner, so no one else would ask questions about the mark on my face. I knew biting wasn't normal behaviour but the thought came into my head that maybe it was all my fault. Maybe I was somehow to blame for the imam doing these strange things to me. I was a bad person. I deserved to be punished. I remembered Mum and Dad saying that if the imam punished you it was for your own good. Was this for my own good? Was it making me a better person?

The following night the imam bit me again. Now I was utterly terrified. The second mark on my face would surely give the game away. Everyone would find out about the dirty things he'd done to me. This time I thought very seriously about telling Mum. The first bite mark had turned into a purple bruise and the second was still livid red and angry-looking. If I showed her the marks on my face, she would have to believe me. I practised in my head the words I would use, but it sounded odd to say, 'The imam bit me.' What if she hit me for telling wicked lies?

I panicked when I heard Habib's footsteps outside the mosque door. I couldn't bear him to see the marks so I pulled at my hair and draped it across the side of my face. I felt ashamed. I desperately wanted to tell Mum, and all the way home I practised the words in my head. But by the time we reached our front door I knew I'd never be able to tell her. I'd die of embarrassment if I had to repeat the strange things the imam had done to me. I thought of the shame it would bring on the family. We'd be cast out of the community, all because of me. The family name would be dragged through the mud. I thought of my lovely father, who would be heartbroken. Mum would be furious with me. She'd say it was all my fault. Maybe it was.

I decided then and there that I couldn't tell anyone. Instead, I'd hide it. I had to protect everyone from this – my friends and my family. I couldn't let this tarnish them. I'd have to keep the secret to myself forever.

As soon as we opened the door, Mum called out to us from the kitchen.

'Dinner won't be long,' she said.

'Okay,' I replied. 'I'm freezing. I'm just going to get warm.'

'I told you to take a coat,' she tutted.

Habib rolled his eyes. 'Nothing to do with me,' he muttered. 'I just pick her up.'

I dashed through to the back room where the fire was roaring away full blast. The room was empty – this was my chance. I held my reddened cheek as close as I could to the bars of the fire. The intense heat seared my skin like meat under a grill. I imagined my beautiful face melting away just like the doll Tariq had destroyed years earlier. If I melted my face then I'd be ugly and the imam wouldn't want me any more. The heat was so strong that I could feel it drying out the liquid from my eyes, nose and mouth within seconds. I stayed like that with my head bent inwards towards the bars of the gas fire until a scream broke the silence.

'Nabila!' Mum shouted from the doorway. 'Get away from the fire! What on earth are you doing?'

She dashed across the room and pulled me away.

I clasped a hand to my face to cover it and my skin felt hot and singed beneath my palm.

'Take your hand away,' Mum scolded, and she grabbed it and leaned forward to have a closer look. She was horrified.

'Why did you do that? You could have burnt yourself and your hair ... your hair could have gone up like that!' She clicked her fingers dramatically.

'Sorry, Mum,' I replied.

'Does it hurt?'

I shook my head. It did, but I wasn't going to tell her that because it would only make her worse.

'What am I going to do with you, Nabila? How many times do I have to tell you not to sit too close to the fire?'

She pushed past me and twisted the brown dial on top of the fire, clicking it off. She was upset and angry with me.

I wanted to weep. I wanted to tell my mum that I was trying to burn my face so I could hide the imam's bites. I felt horrible, soiled. I just wanted to be a little girl again.

I was convinced that Mum would tell Dad about the fire, but she didn't. Instead, she shook her head sadly at me over the dinner table that night. I pulled my hair protectively around my face, feeling stupid and silly. My long hair came in handy because from now on I'd use it as a shield to hide behind. I wanted to hide the dirty, smelly, useless child I'd become. The imam had made me feel like a piece of rubbish – dirty, used up and broken. No one would want to know me now, not if they discovered my secret.

At school the next day my friends asked about the strange oval-shaped bruise on my cheek.

I self-consciously pulled my hair around my face as I replied, 'I sat too close to the gas fire.' Everyone believed me. I was becoming so good at lying that I almost believed myself these days.

Not long after that I happened to overhear a group of older girls talking about love bites in the playground, and I sidled up so that I was near enough to listen. One of the girls said that a boy had tried to give her one.

'Is it like Dracula does?' someone asked, and the girl laughed.

'No, they don't really bite. They suck – like this.' She demonstrated on the back of her hand. 'See?' she said, holding it out for us all to look at. 'It makes a red mark. Sometimes it makes a bruise. My mum says they're cheap and any girl who has one is a tart.'

Now I knew what the strange bite was. A love bite. What a peculiar name for it. To me on the receiving end, it didn't feel as though there was anything loving about it at all.

Every day when the school bell rang at three-thirty my heart sank. In an hour and a half I'd be back at the mosque. In some ways I was prepared for it – at least I knew what to expect – but I didn't dread it any less.

The walk there was long and lonely. The traffic whizzed by me and I wondered what would happen if I just slipped off the kerb and stepped out in front of a car. My life would be over in a moment. I wondered if anyone would really miss me. I felt sad thinking of my lovely mum and dad because they'd be heartbroken. I pictured Mum crying herself to sleep at night after I'd died and guilt overwhelmed me. How could I even think such a wicked thing? Mum had waited so long for a little girl. She'd almost lost me before I was born, and now I wanted to end my life. I was a selfish, horrible little girl. I had to get through this. I just had to do what the imam said until at last I was allowed to leave the mosque.

Every evening he was waiting for me as I pushed open the door, and straight away he beckoned me up to his room. I climbed each step slowly, as if it were my last.

'We need to practise your reading,' he would say, studying me from his chair.

I always tried standing away from him at the edge of the desk but he would grab my waist roughly and pull me over. 'You need to be close enough to see the book, don't you?'

He stroked my sore cheek and leaned in close so I could smell his rancid breath near my mouth. My lips trembled and my eyes watered. I was perpetually terrified that he was going to bite me again. I flinched every time I felt his hot steamy breath against my skin. He lifted his hand away from my waist and began to caress my back and bum.

'Read, pretty girl,' he kept saying. 'Go on, read.'

I began to speak, tracing the words on the page with my finger so that I wouldn't lose my place. My head was buzzing, my senses on full alert, wondering what he'd do to me next. My eyes were always following the clock on the office wall, counting the minutes until the others would arrive. If I could get through this, then I'd be fine.

Soon he wasn't content with stroking my back and bum. One night he started to slide his hand round to my belly and inch up towards my breasts. I wriggled to try and make him stop but he grasped my right breast in his hand and squeezed hard. A sharp pain shot through me and I winced and pulled away. My breasts were tender and the imam's hands were rough.

'What's the matter, pretty girl? Don't you like to be touched?' he leered.

The more I backed away, the more he clung onto me. 'What's wrong with you? This is fun! Doesn't it feel good?'

I wanted to spit in his face as he grabbed at my body, his dirty fingernails digging deep into my flesh. I cried out with pain.

'Did I hurt you?' he asked in mock concern. 'Sorry, next time I'll be more gentle.'

With that he grabbed the back of my head and forced my face to his. I squeezed my lips tight together as he approached me with his mouth open, showing his rotting brown teeth. I shut my eyes and gagged as he rammed his tongue deep into my mouth, filling it up. He wiggled his tongue around. I couldn't breathe so I snorted through my nose. Just at that moment he pulled sharply away and wiped his mouth with the back of his hand. He adjusted his sarong over his private parts and turned away from me abruptly, as if he was almost angry.

'Your work is done. Go downstairs and wait for the others.'

I didn't need to be told twice. I was free! I dashed down the steps, back to the toilet and the soap. The bar was mashed and grimy but I needed to get the taste of him out of my mouth so I shoved the whole thing inside and moved it around before spitting it out. The chemical smell made me gag and my eyes watered as I rubbed a soapy finger right round my gums. I had to wash him off me, wash him clean out of my mouth. I cupped my hands together and filled them with cold water, then I sucked it in and swilled it around before spitting it out. The taste made me retch. I cupped some water and swilled again. But I wasn't done yet.

I lifted my top and rubbed the cold water over my breasts, where he had touched me. It dripped down my stomach, soaking the waistband of my trousers.

Next I scrubbed hard at my hands, washing them over and over again. I splashed my face and dragged my hands slowly over it, sniffing at them. I didn't want to smell of him. I couldn't bear to smell of the dirty imam.

Afterwards, the taste of the soap was in my mouth all evening and it was still there when I went to bed that night. I didn't want to be his pretty girl any more. I prayed that soon it could be someone else's turn because I didn't think I could bear it much longer.

Chapter 10

Treasure under the Carpet

The imam's behaviour at the mosque was always on my mind, both at school and at home, filling all my waking hours. My ninth birthday passed, and still it went on. Five nights a week I had to see him, and my only respite was at weekends. It didn't matter how much I dragged my feet or took detours on the way to the mosque, because if there wasn't enough time before the children arrived he'd wait until afterwards. Habib had been picking me up later and later and was never there before eight o'clock, while the very last of the other children would be out of the door by seven-thirty. The imam had at least half an hour to do as he wanted with me.

One night he asked me to sit on his lap.

Something inside me snapped and I shook my head in defiance. I hadn't thought it through. It was just an instinctive revulsion to the idea. 'I don't want to,' I said, as firmly as I could, although my legs were trembling.

'But I am your teacher – you must do as I tell you,' he insisted, his face flushed with anger.

I was terrified. I didn't want to sit on his lap but I didn't want to make him cross either. I remembered him beating that boy with a stick and didn't want it to happen to me.

'Please don't make me,' I said quietly, my voice shaking. 'I don't want to.'

'Come on,' he said, pulling me by the hand towards him. 'Sit and read.'

He tapped his lap, and when he saw that I wasn't going to climb on voluntarily he grabbed me and lifted me onto it. His sarong slipped about underneath my cotton trousers and I could feel the warmth of his bare thighs. Fear made me freeze to the spot. I sat as still and cold as a porcelain statue. If I stayed still then perhaps he would forget I was there. His breath smelt of spices and unbrushed teeth; it smelt of decay. He stroked my face and sighed fondly.

'You're so lovely, a lovely little girl. A very pretty girl.' His voice trailed off to a whisper as he began to kiss my face and neck.

I looked straight ahead and focused on a dirty stain on the wall in front of me. It was shaped like a cute puppy dog with a button nose, big eyes and ears that flopped down at the side. I concentrated on the shapes and the picture in my head. If I looked hard enough then I'd be able to forget that I was here, with the dirty old imam, and imagine I was playing with the puppy.

The imam's hands slid up and down my body on top of my clothes. The odour from his armpits was leaking out, like poison emanating from underneath his skin.

'So beautiful,' he murmured, as he nuzzled into my neck.

I glanced at the large white clock on the wall: only five more minutes of this and Habib would be here. I watched the second hand as it ticked slowly around the clock face.

The imam squeezed my face. I remained motionless. If he saw I wasn't enjoying it then maybe he'd stop, I reasoned.

'So pretty.'

He began to suck and lick at my face and neck. I screwed my face up in disgust. It felt horrible, his big rubbery tongue sliding along my skin like a fat snake. I prayed for it to stop, but it didn't. The imam grunted as he bit at my skin. Pain shot through me and my eyes brimmed with tears. Soon I was crying, the tears flooding down my face and neck onto his mouth and lips. He didn't seem to notice, and if he did he didn't care. To him I was just a pretty little object. I had no feelings.

The mosque door creaked open downstairs. When I heard it I jumped straight off his lap. Habib was here. I didn't ask to leave. I just ran out without looking back. Behind me I could hear the imam's laughter ringing in my ears. He knew I'd never dare say anything – he knew his dirty secret was safe with me.

'Sorry I'm late,' Habib said once we were outside. 'But look, I've brought you something.' He held out a Wispa chocolate bar. It was my favourite and it made me want to cry. Habib had done something kind for me and he'd apologised for being late. It was almost unprecedented. Of course, he didn't want me to tell Mum that he'd been late picking me up, so this was a bribe. He didn't realise that his lateness had left me in the arms of a monster, and there was no way I could tell him.

I bit into the bar and savoured the taste of the velvety chocolate melting against my tongue. Wispas had always been my favourite. However, I'd rather have had him collect me from the mosque on time than have all the chocolate in the world.

Asif had told me that Habib had a girlfriend at college. We kids all knew, but Mum and Dad didn't. He seemed keen on her and it meant he got later and later every night because he wanted to spend as much time as possible with her. He'd arrive at the mosque out of breath from running all the way from college.

'You won't tell Mum I was late tonight, will you?' he asked as we walked along.

'Nope,' I promised.

'Good girl,' Habib smiled, patting me on the head. I flinched as he did it. I was so used to the imam touching me that now I automatically moved away at the slightest touch.

'What's wrong with you?' he complained. 'I was just trying to be nice.'

I thought Mum might say something about the fact that we were so late home for dinner, but she never batted an eyelid. She seemed to want me to be out of the house as much as possible and didn't like it when I hung around 'getting under her feet'. When we got home she'd just serve up our dinner without another word.

She always seemed preoccupied. I supposed it was running a big house and looking after five children that kept her so busy.

A few weeks later, the imam called me up to his room but when I walked through the door he wasn't sitting in his usual chair. Instead he was flicking through some books at the bookcase.

'You need to do some cleaning,' he instructed. 'Start with my toilet, then do the kitchen.'

I nodded and went to fetch cleaning fluid from the kitchen. I scrubbed at his toilet until it gleamed before going back into the kitchen to wash all the dirty dishes. I worked hard, standing with my back to the side of the sink so that I could keep an eye on the door.

After a while the imam called me into his office. My heart sank; he'd want me to 'read' for him, I just knew it. But when I entered the room he wasn't in his usual place at the desk. Instead he was standing over in the corner, by the bed.

'Come here,' he whispered. 'I've got something to show you.' He pointed downwards.

I froze in the doorway. Whatever it was, I didn't want to see it.

The imam looked surprised, then his face broke into a huge smile.

'Don't worry, I'm not going to hurt you,' he began. 'I just wondered whether you like jewellery and precious things.'

I was puzzled but I nodded and said 'yes' in a quiet little voice, then I got scared that it might be a trick question.

The imam grinned. 'And do you like treasure?'

I nodded my head again, thinking about the cartoons I watched on TV. I loved cartoons with pirates, especially when they stole treasure chests full of gold coins and took them back to their caves. I pictured a large wooden box with gold goblets and precious jewels spilling out of it. I glanced around his filthy bedroom, sure there was no treasure there.

'I have some hidden treasure to show you,' the imam said.

He turned his back to me and knelt down on the floor. I could see him pulling at something and wondered what it was. Curiosity got the better of me and I wandered over and tried to sneak a peek over his shoulder. He felt me behind him and spun around, making me jump back with surprise. I was scared it was a trick and that he was going to grab me any moment, but he didn't. Instead, he tugged at the edge of the carpet and peeled it away from the wooden gripper board. Little metal teeth ripped open as he forced it back, pushing the carpet with his foot.

'If you want to see treasure,' he said, 'look underneath the carpet.' He flung out his arm to show me.

In a cavity in the bare floorboards there was money – heaps of it – all in coins. It glinted and shone in the light from the bulb on the ceiling. I'd never seen so much money in my life. There were ten-pence pieces, fifty-pence pieces, and hundreds of one- and two-pence coins. There were coins of every size and colour. But there, right in the middle, sat the most precious of all – a gold one pound coin. They'd recently come out. I'd seen one

on TV but I'd never seen a real one before. I gasped
when I spotted it. The imam noticed this and chuckled.

'Do you want that one?' he asked, pointing at the
gold coin.

I looked at him in disbelief. A whole pound to myself
– I'd never had so much money before in my life. I'd be
rich! My eyes widened as I imagined all the sweets I'd
be able to buy.

'But look, Nabila,' he said. 'There are lots of them.'

I glanced along at the edge of the skirting board, and
saw he was right; there were lots of little gold coins all
lined up – so many in fact that I couldn't count them all.

He picked up a one-pound coin and held it out to
me.

'Take it,' he insisted. 'It's yours.'

I plucked the coin from his outstretched palm. It was
heavy in my fingers as I turned it over again and again
in my hand. It was pretty and shiny. I loved it and
wanted to keep it.

'You are a hard worker. You are a good girl,' the
imam said. 'Any time you need money, you come in
here and help yourself. Now you know where the treasure is hidden, you can take it any time you want and
spend it on yourself.' He leaned over and stroked my
head.

'Just lift up the carpet. But Nabila,' he warned,
putting a finger to his lips, 'this is our secret, okay? You
mustn't tell anyone where the treasure is hidden.'

I nodded. I wouldn't tell a soul.

When it was time to go home I walked over to the
mosque door and collected my shoes. I held one in my

hand and secretly let the coin drop down into it. I pushed my foot into the shoe, shunting the coin to the end with my big toe. No one would ever find it there.

It was uncomfortable walking home with the coin in my shoe. It rubbed against my toes, making me limp slightly, but Habib didn't notice. He was far too busy with his own life to worry about his little sister.

Still, I had a gold coin all of my own. What I didn't realise was that by taking the money I'd taken payment for what the imam was doing to me. It was a wage to buy my silence. That coin was mine, but in return I'd paid a very high price. I'd paid for it with my innocence.

Chapter 11

The Trip to the Petrol Station

As soon as I got home I ran to my bedroom and pulled the gold pound coin from my shoe. It was still shiny and beautiful, but I knew I had to hide it. If Mum found it she would want to know where it came from, and there was nothing I could say without giving away what was happening with the imam. And I knew I couldn't do that.

My eyes scanned the room looking for a hiding place and I spotted my pink pencil case on the dressing table. It was a spare, not the one I took to school, so it would be perfect. No one would ever think to look in there. I unfastened the little magnets that ran across the top and opened the case, then pushed the coin deep down underneath my pencils, pens and rubbers. I clicked the magnets together again, placed it back on the side and smiled to myself. I had a small fortune. I was rich and no one even knew.

I kept the coin in my pencil case for the next two weeks, glancing in every morning and evening to check it was still there. Then I began to feel anxious that Mum might still find it so I hid the pencil case under some of my clothes in a drawer. I couldn't think what to do with it because if I spent it on sweets Mum would wonder where I'd got the money for them. Gradually I began to see my treasure as a problem rather than a reward.

'Take more treasure,' the imam would tell me. 'Whenever you want, you take treasure.'

I never took any more coins, though, because I couldn't think what to do with the first one.

One morning I awoke to hear an almighty commotion downstairs. Mum was shouting at Asif, her voice angry and accusing. 'I know you stole it. You took it from my purse. I found it in your clothes, you wicked, wicked boy!'

'But I didn't take it!' he wailed, sounding upset. 'It wasn't me. I don't know how it got there.'

Mum yelled back at him: 'Liar! You are a liar as well as a thief.'

I ran to the top of the stairs. Saeed was coming up and he passed me on the landing.

'What's going on?' I asked.

'Oh, it's Asif,' he said. 'He's stolen a pound from Mum's purse and she says she's gonna tell Dad.'

Saeed rolled his eyes and grimaced. Dad would be furious if he found out. Asif would be grounded, probably for the rest of his life. Stealing was something he felt very strongly about.

I ran back into my bedroom to get dressed. Suddenly I remembered the pound coin hidden in my pencil case. If Mum ever found it she would think I had stolen it from her. She would accuse me, just as she was accusing Asif.

My heart raced as I considered what to do next. I shut my bedroom door and slipped the pound coin out of the pencil case. My eyes flitted around the room anxiously. I needed to find another hiding place, but nowhere would be entirely safe. No matter where I put it, Mum might find it when she cleaned my room. If she found it she'd demand to know where it came from, and I'd have to tell her that the horrible imam gave it to me. I couldn't contemplate that. She would be so upset with me. She'd accuse me of lying and making up stories and I couldn't bear to think what would happen after that. I decided that I'd have to spend the money as soon as possible to get rid of the evidence. My black school shoes were on the floor under the radiator. I pushed the coin deep inside the toe of one of them. I'd carry it around with me all day at school and spend it on the way to the mosque that night.

The hard edge of the coin rubbed against my toe as I limped all the way to school. I couldn't run around in the playground as usual because my toe was hurting. I limped home at three-thirty, then set out to the mosque after four. I took a different route that evening, past the petrol station further down the main road. It was where Dad always bought his petrol and the man in the shop knew me well. I hesitated just outside the shop door-way, worrying that he might mention to Dad that I'd been there, but there were no other shops in the area. If I didn't spend the coin there I'd have to hide it for another day and Mum might find it. I scratched my head. It seemed I had no choice.

I pulled off my shoe and let the pound coin drop into my palm then put my shoe back on and crept into the shop.

The man behind the counter recognised me straight away.

'Hello, Smiler!' he chirped. 'How are you doing?'

He'd always called me 'Smiler' since I was little.

'She's got such a lovely smile,' he'd say to Dad. 'She's such a pretty little thing.' Unlike the imam, he never tried to touch me, though.

He was in his forties, same as Dad, and had a Filipino wife who was about twenty years younger. She would move around in the background, silently stacking the shelves, but whenever she saw me she would always give me a big smile.

'What can I get you today, little lady?' the petrol station man asked.

'Err, some sweets please.' I pointed behind him at the jars of confectionery on the shelf.

'Which ones?'

I held the pound coin in my palm. It was sweaty and I worried about handing it over to him. What if it smelt of stinky feet after a whole day inside my shoe?

I looked back at the jars. I needed to spend this money quickly so I chose the biggest sweets I could see.

'The red bubblegums, please.'

The man lifted the jar from the shelf, opened a white paper bag and looked at me. 'How many?'

I hadn't thought of that. I didn't even know how much they cost, so I said the first number that came into my head – not too big and not too small. 'Twenty please.'

'That many? Are you sure?' He began to count them into the bag. 'You want to be careful. You'll have no teeth left after eating so many of these. You don't want to lose that lovely smile of yours, do you?' He gave me a wink.

I began to panic. Was twenty too many? Would he tell my dad?

'I'm sharing them with my friends,' I explained weakly.

The man twisted the bag shut and handed it over to me. I placed the pound coin in his hand and waited for him to ask me why I had so much money. *'How come a little girl like you is so rich?'* But he didn't say a word. He just took the coin from me and keyed the amount into the till. It beeped loudly.

I turned to walk away.

'Hang on a minute!' he called.

I froze to the spot. I'd been rumbled, I just knew it.

'Your change! You've forgotten your change!'

I turned back towards the counter. I hadn't realised that there'd be change. As the man let the coins drop into my hand, I gasped. Before I'd only had one coin, but now there were lots. He counted out eighty pence in loose change. I had no idea where I would hide it all. For the time being I had to slip it inside my shoes and I could hear it jangling as I continued the rest of the way to the mosque.

The mosque bus was already there when I arrived and the children were spilling off it. Thank goodness I'd managed to be late enough to avoid being alone with the imam this time. Farqad noticed me and came dashing over.

'What's in the bag?' she asked.

'Bubblegum. Do you want one?' I held out the bag, scrunching my toes over the coins to stop them from rattling around.

Within minutes I was surrounded by children, like a pack of wolves drooling over a plump chicken. They'd spotted the sweets and now they all wanted some. I handed the bag around, enjoying the feeling of being able to share with the others. It made me feel popular again. I was the girl with the sweets and suddenly everyone wanted to be my friend. I didn't even have any bubblegum myself because it was all gone by the time the bag got back to me. That was fine. I hadn't really wanted any.

Inside the mosque, I pushed the loose change further into the toes of my shoes and placed them with the others by the door, hoping that no one would pick them up by mistake.

The following night I bought a huge bag full of gobstoppers, which were more expensive than bubblegum. The other children were delighted when I handed them round.

'What have you got tonight?' the boys asked, crowding around.

After that I went to the petrol station every night on my way to the mosque and bought more and more sweets until the money had gone. I liked the popularity they bought me. I liked the way the other children came rushing over as soon as I arrived.

'Have you got sweets, have you got sweets?'

Even the girls who had been mean to me and said I thought I was something special were being friendly to me now. I was buying their friendship with sweets bought from money given to me by the evil imam. I wondered how shocked they'd be if I told them all about his wandering hands and his disgusting kisses and bites. I could never tell them about the treasure he kept hidden underneath the carpet in his bedroom. I needed friends at the mosque to give me strength when I sat through the lessons, my dread growing as the moment approached when everyone else left and we would be on our own.

Once the money was finished, I considered taking more. The imam had said I could take as much as I wanted, but I decided against it. It was dirty money. It was a bribe with which he hoped to buy my silence, so it was tainted in my eyes, even if it did have the positive effect of making the other children friendly towards me. I worried that they would stop being my friend when I didn't have sweets any more, but they were much nicer than they had been before.

One day it dawned on me where the imam's treasure had come from. Each night he asked the children to remind their parents that he needed donations to keep the mosque going. The children would bring in loose change and hand it over. When I glanced into the box where the change was kept, it looked exactly the same as the treasure, with a mixture of different denominations of coins all jumbled up together. I guessed that's where all the money under the carpet came from. Instead of using the donations for the upkeep of the mosque, the imam was keeping at least some of it for himself. That's why it was hidden under the carpet – because he was a thief. He stole money from the mosque, he told lies and he touched little girls. He was a bad person and I couldn't understand why anyone would let him be a religious leader, a teacher of young people, and head of the community. It seemed all wrong to me.

Upstairs in his office he continued to touch me in even more strange and horrible ways. Now he would always force me to sit on his lap as I read the day's lesson from the Koran. While I was reading he tried to lift my top to touch my breasts, but I wrestled it down again and instead he touched them over the top of the fabric. He stroked the inside of my thigh and his hand moved up to touch my private parts between my legs. No one had ever touched me down there before – no one. I knew for sure it was dirty and wrong. He shouldn't be doing it and I shouldn't be letting him, but I had nowhere to run and hide. He was in control, not me. He had the power. It was all done in the context of a lesson about the Koran. I had to keep reading the words on the page, no matter how much my voice was trembling.

'You've pronounced that bit wrong,' he leered, as he continued to stroke me down below. 'Read it again.'

His beard was hot and itchy against my face as he licked my cheek. All the time his hand continued to stroke me down below, making me feel very weird. My head was whirring. Sometimes I could feel something hard poking into me through the cloth of my trousers, like a pen of some kind. I had no idea what it was, but I knew I didn't like it. I hated the heat, the smell, the touch – I hated everything about him.

I'd feel self-conscious as I joined the other children downstairs. I worried that I must look different somehow. I felt dirty and embarrassed by what I'd been doing with the imam and wondered if it was obvious and if they could somehow read the guilty shame on my face. I was terrified that they would find out. They'd all think I was filthy and smelly, just like the imam. I felt as though he'd made me as horrible and dirty as him. The children would hate me for it. Adults wouldn't believe me and I'd be punished for telling lies. My family would all be shamed and cast out of the community. The children would think I was rotten and dirty and would steer well clear of me. No one would ever want to be my friend again, no matter how many sweets I bought them.

I vowed that no one could ever find out – I'd rather die than let that happen. I had to keep this secret to myself until the day I died.

Chapter 12

A Lost Innocence

I wasn't safe if I got to the mosque early and I definitely wasn't safe after the last child left at seven-thirty when I was alone with the imam until Habib arrived, but I'd always thought I was safe in the period in between when everyone was sitting doing their lessons. However, one day the imam called me to the little table at the front of the mosque and told me to sit down and recite my prayers. In front of me, seventy children sat reading their own prayer books.

Everyone dreaded having to read for the imam like this because the slightest mispronunciation or hesitation over a word could earn you a slap. Of course, he had never slapped me but there could always be a first time. I sat on the floor where he indicated, crossed my legs and shuffled closer to the prayer table so I could rest my prayer book on it. He was kneeling on the other side of the table, and as I sat I caught a glimpse of his black underpants. My heart lurched and I gave a shudder.

I focused on the prayer book instead, trying not to think about the horrible lap he made me sit on up in the office and the nasty stains I'd seen in those black underpants. I started reciting the prayer, taking great care with my pronunciation because I didn't want to get it wrong. I didn't want to spend a second longer than necessary close to him.

Suddenly I felt a hot clammy hand slide under the table and up around the inside of my thigh. The breath caught in the back of my throat. Had anyone seen what he'd just done? I scanned the room but all the kids had their heads bowed and were deep in prayer. Even if they did look up, the table would shield his hands from sight. I breathed out. No one had noticed – my secret was safe, for now. I couldn't bear for anyone to find out. I'd die of shame if they did. My family would hate me and so would everyone else. Everyone respected the imam but no one respected me. They'd all blame me and not him.

The imam shuffled closer until his knees were almost touching mine. It gave his wandering hands even more scope to rub up the inside of my thigh, as high as he could reach, until he was almost touching my private parts. I jerked backwards.

'*No, not here, not now. Please.*' The words swam around my head. I was looking at him, my eyes pleading with him to stop, but he just smirked and continued to touch me. He was letting me know that he was in control, even here, even now, in front of all these children. There were no hiding places. I wasn't safe here or anywhere else. He could grab and grope me whenever or wherever he chose to, whether we were alone or in a room full of people. The imam was so powerful that he could do this horrible thing to me whenever he wanted to. I'd just have to suffer in silence.

I struggled through the prayer as best I could. I knew I was making lots of mistakes but he didn't comment on them. When I got to the end he told me that I'd done well and was free to go. I jumped to my feet like a startled animal and rushed back to my place and the safety of my friend.

Farqad was looking at me oddly, and for a moment I thought she must have seen. She leaned over to whisper to me. 'Why does he always let you off when you make mistakes? You don't know how lucky you are.'

'*Lucky!*' I thought. '*If only she knew the truth, she wouldn't be saying that.*'

I thought the prayer table incident would be a one-off, but I was wrong. Every time he called me out to read for him he'd do it again. It got to the point when I just sat there waiting for it to happen. It didn't matter how many people were in the room because he knew that I wouldn't say anything and that they wouldn't notice. He had absolute power over me. He'd got away with it once and now the thrill of watching me squirm seemed to excite him even more. I was the puppet and he was the puppeteer, the one who pulled all the strings. I hated it and him. I was his cleaner and his plaything and there was nothing I could do about it.

I'd intended to learn the Koran as quickly as possible so that I could leave the mosque forever, but the strain of the constant abuse meant that I struggled to concentrate on my prayers and fell further and further behind with my religious studies. I feared this would mean that I'd have to stay at the mosque forever. My hands were tied.

And always I lived with the fear of being discovered. The imam continued to suck and bite me, leaving telltale bruises that it was difficult to hide, and they became a mark of my shame. In a bid to conceal them I became a master of disguise. I'd use my hair and my hands to cover them whenever someone spoke to me. In the mosque I pulled my headscarf forwards until my face almost disappeared inside it, and at home I'd play with strands of hair, pulling them across my cheeks.

'What's that mark on your face?' Mum asked one evening over the dinner table.

Everyone turned towards to me and I flushed red at the attention, instinctively covering the latest sore with my hand. Mum grabbed my hand and pulled it away, leaning forward for a closer look at the mark.

'It's nothing,' I protested, and with my other hand I pinched my cheek to make it look as though that might have caused the bruising.

'Stop it!' Mum scolded, slapping my hands away. 'Why do you do these things? Why do you damage your face in this way?'

The room fell silent as Mum waited for an answer, but I didn't have one. Instead I just shrugged my shoulders, which infuriated her more.

'You've changed, Nabila, and I don't like it.
You used to be sweet and bubbly and chatty and
now you are sullen and moody. I don't know what's
going on, but whatever it is I want you to snap out of
it.'

'*I'll tell you why I'm moody,*' I thought. '*I've been
being abused for two and a half years now by the imam
at the mosque and there's nothing I can do about it.*'

The days when I used to laugh and joke with my
family were a distant memory from a long time ago. I
never smiled any more. Any confidence I'd ever
possessed had been destroyed by the imam. Now I felt
nervous and frightened almost the whole time.

Subconsciously I started pinching my cheek again,
and Dad joined in. 'Nabila, stop that at once.' He
pointed in my direction with his fork. 'Leave your face
alone.'

Before this I'd always been the good girl of the family,
perfectly behaved in comparison to my four brothers.
But I wasn't good any more. Instead, I was dirty and
bad. The imam had made me feel bad and now that
badness had stolen away my voice. I didn't dare speak
just in case bad things came out of my mouth. He'd
robbed me of everything. I wasn't important any more.
It was easier to be quiet and fade into the background.
The imam had picked me out from the rest, and that's
when all the trouble started. That's why I didn't want
to be noticed by anyone now. Being noticed only made
bad things happen.

I lowered my head and tried to eat although each
mouthful of food lodged in my throat. It was impossible

to swallow. Could they tell the mark on my face was a love bite? I was burning up with shame.

Mum made a tutting noise, a noise of disgust. I disgusted her. The family continued to eat their meal and I tried my best to finish my food, but my stomach felt as though it held the rough waves of the sea inside it. It churned with anxiety. Would there be more awkward questions that I didn't have the answer to? Thankfully, there weren't.

That evening, as I got undressed for bed, there was a quiet knock at my bedroom door. I opened it to find Tariq standing there.

'Why *is* your face always marked?' he asked.

I shrugged my shoulders; I didn't know what to say.

'If anyone's picking on you, you'd tell me, wouldn't you?'

I nodded my head and looked down at the floor. I was certain that if he looked into my eyes he'd be able to see the truth about what I'd been up to with the imam.

'No one's picking on me. It's just …' my voice tailed off, as I desperately tried to think up a reason for the marks. 'It's just I get bored and I pick and pull at my skin sometimes. I do it without thinking.'

Tariq looked at me as if he didn't believe me.

'It's the mosque,' I said suddenly, the words spilling out of my mouth.

In that moment I longed to tell Tariq. I remembered the way he had punched the other imam and knocked him to the ground. He wasn't scared of imams. Surely if I told him what this one was doing he would charge down there, beat up the imam and rescue me. He'd sort the imam out. All I had to do was say the word and I'd be free of the evil imam and his dirty ways.

But I couldn't tell my brother. If I told him it would then become Tariq's shame and the shame of the entire family. How could I bring shame on them like that? I couldn't do it.

'It's the mosque …' I continued. 'It's just so boring. I pick at my face for something to do, you know, to pass the time.'

What was I thinking? I'd almost let the cat out of the bag. I looked at his face to see if he'd twigged, but his expression didn't change. He studied me for a moment longer.

'Well, OK then,' he replied, 'but if someone's picking on you, or bullying you in any way, I want you to tell me. Promise you will?'

'Yes,' I said. 'Don't worry about me. I suppose I'm just a little odd – that's all.' I laughed and rolled my eyes.

Tariq gave me one more searching look, before turning to go back downstairs.

A sob caught in my throat. I wanted to call him back and tell him the truth. I still could. But the words were locked away, deep down inside me. I couldn't let this secret go. Now I'd have to carry it around with me, like a dark stain on my heart. I knew then that the imam would always be there, that he'd always be in control. This would be my dirty little secret forever.

That night I cried myself to sleep. Tariq was trying to be kind; he was trying to protect me. Not being able to tell him my problems made me feel more alone than ever before.

My primary-school teacher began to ask me some searching questions. I'd always liked my teacher and tried my best to do well for her, but now I had no concentration in class. I'd stare at the blackboard but instead of seeing the words I'd be worrying about going to the mosque later on. When the teacher asked me a question I'd be unable to answer it because my thoughts were miles away.

She asked me to stay behind after class one day and was so kind that I almost told her what was on my mind. She taught us religious studies, among other subjects, so she would be able to say once and for all whether it was OK for the imam to be biting and kissing and touching me. She would know if it was against the rules.

I stood in front of her and looked into her kind, concerned face and I desperately wanted to tell her, but I simply couldn't think of what words to use. Tears came to my eyes.

'Is everything all right at home?' she asked.

I nodded, biting my lip.

'Are any of your friends being mean to you?'

I shook my head. How could I say it? *The imam bites me. He touches me and kisses me.* I nearly said it, but then my courage failed me.

The teacher looked disappointed. 'I know something's wrong and I wish you would tell me, Nabila. Remember I'm always here.'

But I couldn't tell her, and after a while she stopped asking. I think she assumed I had simply lost interest in my schoolwork. I sensed she was disappointed in me, and that made me feel even worse. But my over-riding emotion was still fear of the shame if anyone found out my secret.

The imam's love bites were a visible reminder of him but I began to worry about other signs as well. Would anyone smell his foul scent on my skin? I began washing myself incessantly after I had been with him. When I got home at night I'd dash straight to the bathroom, lock the door and wash myself all over. There was a big bar of Imperial Leather soap beside the sink. I'd seen adverts on TV in which a beautiful woman rubbed it all over her skin. But I didn't want to be beautiful; I just wanted to be plain and normal. I dug my fingernails deep into the soap then scoured them across my face. I wanted to spread the bruise out and make it disappear, but it didn't work. Now, as well as a bruise, I had long red scratch marks all down my cheeks. I looked as if I'd been clawed by a cat. Afterwards, my skin would feel even sorer but at least it was clean and tight as a new drum.

I'd brush my teeth too, obsessively scouring them until they were sparkling. His teeth were rotten and black, just like his soul. The thought of the imam's spit in my mouth made me want to gag so I scrubbed any traces of his saliva from my tongue. I brushed and brushed and kept brushing until my gums bled.

Whenever Mum was out of the room I'd sit close to the fire to try and burn my skin. I'd always be sure to listen for her footsteps near the door so that I could move away at the last moment. The skin on my face would smart and burn with the heat but it felt good, as though I was melting his marks away and purifying myself again. I worked out that if I knelt with my back to the settee where Mum was sitting, I could get close enough to the fire as we watched TV without her even noticing.

One cold and wintry evening, when the wind and rain were lashing outside, Mum nagged me to wear extra layers when I went to the mosque. 'Put on your heavy top and trousers and your jumper,' she called upstairs to me, 'and don't forget to wear a coat!'

I hoped the extra-thick clothing would keep the imam's horrible hot hands away from me for once, but instead it had the opposite effect. He seemed to see it as a challenge. I squirmed on his lap as he held me tight and forced his hands under the waistband of my trousers and down into my pants. It was the first time he'd touched me under my clothes like that. My body stiffened with fear. Putting your hands in someone's pants was horrible and wrong. I was so petrified that I held my breath. The imam began twirling his fingers around against my private parts, hurting me, and he grunted loudly in my ear.

I shut my eyes and tried to think about nice things. I pictured my beautiful dolls. I remembered playing the musical instruments in Suki's prayer room. I saw myself running with my friends in the playground at school. I dreamt of running as fast as I could across the playground, over the fields and through the streets. I saw myself running and running for miles and miles until my legs ached and I could run no more. I'd be long

gone, thousands of miles away from here, thousands of
miles away from the imam.

'You enjoy this, Nabila, don't you?' he sighed.

But I didn't. I hated it. I hated his rough, dry fingers;
they rubbed against my skin and made me feel raw and
sore.

I knew what was going on now. He was doing dirty
sex things with me. We hadn't had proper sex education
lessons at school because I was still too young, only just
ten, but I'd overheard the white girls in the playground
talking about it. I'd listened in horror to their accounts
of how boys would try to do dirty sex things with you
and I'd sworn to myself that I'd never let any boy do
that to me. In my community, no man was supposed to
touch you inside your pants until you were married. But
that's what the imam was doing with me. He was doing
dirty sex. Only tarts let boys do it to them, a girl had
said, so that meant I must be a tart. He had made me
dirty. I felt soiled and used. I'd had my own personal
sex education lesson in the imam's stinking bedroom
and it had made me grow up fast, before I was ready. I
wished I could be a little girl again, inviting friends
round to play with my dollies, but he had taken all that
away from me and I could never go back.

At that moment I felt as though he had destroyed me
and I resolved never to say my prayers again. What was
the point? No god was ever going to come and rescue
me. I hated the imam with a passion. I wished that he
would die a horrible and agonising death. I dreamed of
killing him. I plotted how I'd tell Dad and stand back
while my father attacked him with his old butcher's

meat cleaver. I imagined my brothers kicking him to death, Tariq booting him until he was a big, bloodied mess in a stained white sarong lying limply on the ground. My favourite fantasy was to imagine the imam screaming out in terror as my enraged family came for him. I pictured the fear in his eyes – the same fear I felt every night when I walked through the mosque door.

Once he had started putting his hands inside my clothes, there was no stopping him. The very next evening, he pulled me onto his lap again with his rough hands and straight away he snaked his fingers down inside my pants.

'Please don't,' I whimpered. 'Please stop.'

But the imam wasn't listening. Instead he pushed his hand down further. Suddenly, I felt his finger jabbing hard against my private parts.

'Don't! Please!' I cried, even louder, but the imam ignored my pleas.

Then I felt a horrible pain as though I was being ripped apart. I screamed, trying desperately to work out what he had done. I struggled with all my might to get away but he held me even tighter, breathing hard. The pain was excruciating and it made my entire body shudder.

'Stop!' I begged. 'It hurts too much.'

I began to sob and turned my head to look him in the face, to appeal to any humanity he had left, but his eyes were glazed and unfocused.

'But you like it, don't you, Nabila?' he breathed. 'Doesn't it feel good?'

'No, I don't,' I sobbed.

The more I tried to pull myself away the tighter he held me and the harder he jabbed at me with that rough finger. The pain was deep inside my belly and I realised what had happened. He had somehow put his filthy finger right inside me. I thought of the dirt under his fingernails scratching away against my insides, his filth poisoning me down below. I was terrified that I'd catch a disease from the dirt and become ill. The thought swam around inside my mind. What if I got ill from this? How on earth would I explain that to Mum and Dad?

From then on, the imam stuck his finger inside me every time we were together. I tried to shut my eyes and pretend I was somewhere else but the pain would jolt me straight back onto his lap and that smelly dark room. I tried to focus on the pattern of the embossed wallpaper on the opposite wall. I tried to see the cute puppy dog but now there were only hideous monsters. My whole world had become a living nightmare.

One night when I got home from the mosque and stripped off to wash upstairs I found blood in my pants. It was terrifying. I thought it must mean he'd somehow damaged me and that I'd never be able to have children of my own now. My private parts throbbed with pain all the time. It was like having a big bruise but on the inside, where no one could see. Only I knew it was there. I had to wash the blood off my pants so Mum didn't see them because then she would know I was doing dirty sex things. My secret would come out.

I only had a hazy idea of female anatomy at the time. I became fascinated with my dolls and used to strip their clothes off to look at their smooth private parts then double myself over in the bath to look at my own. I didn't look the same as the dolls and I became worried that the imam had made me different by touching me. If anyone ever looked down there, I thought they would be able to tell what he had done to me. My understanding was muddled and mostly from those white girls in the playground, but I knew that once you had lost 'it' it was gone forever, and I worried that mine was lost now.

I began wetting the bed every single night, and it made me feel even more disgusting and dirty. No matter how careful I was to wee before bedtime, I'd wake up in a cold sodden patch of smelly urine. I'd have to get up in the morning, flip over the mattress and swap the sheet around so the wet patch was out of sight. To save time, I began sleeping in the top half of my school uniform, leaving my knickers and skirt off. That meant I was already half-dressed in the morning, and could get ready for school on time.

Maybe wearing my uniform in bed was like a security blanket. When I was at school I was safe and protected and the imam couldn't get me. Wearing school uniform made me feel calm, as though everything was OK. It helped me to get to sleep.

Soon I was sleeping on several patches of dried-out wee. The white sheets were stained yellow with urine. I was certain that I smelt but there wasn't time for a bath before school. All I could do was splash the backs of my legs, my bottom and private parts with cold water from the sink in the bathroom. I became obsessed with washing myself every morning. I didn't want my friends to smell the wee or the odour of the dirty imam on me.

'What are you doing in there? Hurry up!'

There were seven of us in the house and only one bathroom so people got impatient if I was in there for too long. Sometimes Dad got so annoyed that he'd bang his fist against the door to hurry me up.

But I had to perform the same rituals every morning, otherwise I'd panic. I needed to hide the evidence from Mum and then I had to wash the smell of urine from my body. On my way to school I'd sniff at my clothes to see if I could smell wee on me from the night before. It became an obsession. Sometimes, if Mum was busy downstairs, I'd sneak into her room and squirt a tiny amount of her perfume onto my bottom or the backs of my legs to mask any smells that washing with cold water hadn't shifted. Of course I never smelt that bad – it was all in my head – but, try as I might, I just couldn't stop worrying about it.

At weekends I helped Mum to do the laundry for the whole household. I'd bunch the offending sheet up in my hands and scrunch it deep into the washing machine when she wasn't looking. Later, I'd breathe a sigh of relief as I watched the clean white sheet blowing around on the washing line outside.

It was just another secret I had to keep.

Chapter 13

The Trip to London

One evening the imam made an announcement: we were going on a trip to see a mosque in London. It was a long way but we'd leave early in the morning and get back late in the evening.

'Tell all your sisters and brothers to come,' he said. 'Everyone's invited.'

Farqad was excited. 'You'll sit next to me on the coach, won't you?' she asked.

'I promise.' I didn't share her excitement, because the trip was to be on a Saturday. Saturdays and Sundays were my days off, when I didn't normally have to see the imam, and the thought of a whole extra day in his company filled me with dread.

When I asked at home, Saeed said he would come along, which was a relief. I'd be safe with one of my big brothers there at least.

Mum made a big bag of keema-spiced mincemeat sandwiches for us and we walked down to the mosque together, arriving at eight a.m. It was a hive of activity, with kids running around and parents busy chatting. Saeed spotted one of his old friends and stopped outside to have a chat with him. The imam noticed me standing alone in the corner and came over.

'Come upstairs, I have something for you,' he whispered in my ear.

My heart sank but I followed him. There were lots of people milling about in the hall below but no one commented on me going upstairs with him. Surely he wouldn't touch me today, not with all these people around and my brother just outside? I was scared that everyone would find out. Then they would know what a horrible and smelly little girl I was.

The imam beckoned me into his bedroom and walked over to lift the carpet in the corner where the treasure was kept.

'I've told you that you can come in here and take some treasure any time you want but you never have. Why is that?' he asked.

I didn't tell him that to me it was dirty money. I would have to get rid of it as quickly as I could because it was evidence of what he was doing to me.

'Here,' he said, scooping a pound coin from the bare floorboard. 'Take this for the trip. You can spend it on sweets.'

I didn't want his money – I didn't want anything from him. But I also didn't want to anger or annoy him, not today, not with all these people around us.

'Thank you,' I replied weakly and took the money from his outstretched palm.

Now I would have to earn it, I supposed. Would he do something disgusting to me then and there, before we went to London?

'Come,' the imam said, 'let's go downstairs to be with the others.'

Utter relief flooded me. It swam through my body, calming my nerves. For once I was off the hook. I hurried down the stairs. The hall was full of giddy chattering children. I felt a tap on my shoulder and turned to see Farqad.

'I've been looking for you. Where have you been?' She hugged me.

I folded my fingers over the coin, wondering where to hide it. Could I slip it into the bag with our sandwiches for the journey? As we boarded the coach, I saw Saeed put it on a shelf above his head. I went up intending to stand on tiptoe and slip the coin inside but then I realised that Saeed would wonder where it had come from. He'd start asking questions I wouldn't be able to answer. I had to get rid of that coin somehow.

I looked at Farqad. 'Do you fancy some sweets?'

Her eyes lit up at the suggestion. We bolted off the coach and ran to a nearby shop, where we handpicked a huge bag of goodies including chocolate bars and strawberry bonbons. We kept choosing more sweets until we had spent the whole pound then we hurried back again, and moments later the coach doors slammed shut and we were on our way.

'Let's eat them all as fast as we can,' I suggested. 'Let's eat until we feel sick!'

Farqad giggled and agreed, and that's what we did. It was good to get rid of all evidence of the imam's money. I hated the burden of it.

The journey to London took so long that we didn't have time to see any of the sights of the city. We just went to the mosque, which was huge – much bigger than the one back home. It had a dome on top and was covered with ornate carvings like a proper palace. Inside, a huge crystal chandelier hung down in the centre. It was very grand indeed.

'This is what a mosque is supposed to look like,' I whispered to Farqad, 'not like our smelly mosque back home.'

Imams from up and down the country came to pray and hold conferences at that mosque, and as I looked around I could see them talking to each other, but I had no respect for them. I had no love for religion any more. When I was younger, all I'd ever wanted was to be a good Muslim girl, but the imam had made me question my faith. He'd tarnished it with his dirty words and stinky kisses. If a holy man could do such things to a little girl, then it seemed to me religion must be wrong and twisted. He had taken away my faith; he'd taken everything from me.

We stayed at the mosque for a couple of hours then went to a nearby park, where we all sat down for lunch. I couldn't eat the sandwiches Mum had made because I still felt sick from all the sweets I'd eaten on the coach.

Farqad wasn't hungry either so we ran off to play on the swings. Farqad pushed me higher and higher and, as I sailed through the air, suddenly I felt free of my worries, just for a moment. The imam was there but he couldn't touch me, not with all these people around. I was safe and, for the first time in ages, I could spend time with my friend and have a laugh. I could be a little girl again. I'd been the imam's prisoner for three years now, but on that day I was free to laugh and play.

In my head I saw the imam's room as a prison cell, the mosque as a prison and the imam as my jailer, but there in London I was in a wide-open space where he couldn't hurt me. I spread my arms out and pretended to fly through the air like a bird. I wanted to breathe in the fresh air, to dance and sing. I didn't have to look over my shoulder because today was different. It was only a few hours' peace but I wanted it to last forever.

Chapter 14

The Sickly
Boy

Not long after the trip to London, a new boy arrived at the mosque. I didn't know it then, but he was to become my saviour for a while.

He looked awkward and uncomfortable standing by the door as his mother chatted to the imam. Soon the mother and the imam were laughing. I watched as the little boy stared glumly at the floor. It was clear he didn't want to be here. Even standing alongside his mother, he looked lonely and apprehensive.

My heart went out to him. I'd been in his position and knew what it felt like to be the outsider. I could tell this little boy didn't want to be thrust into a strange room with dozens of noisy kids he didn't know.

Once his mother had left, I went over with Farqad to say hello.

'My name's Nabila. What's yours?' I asked.

'Hamal,' he replied.

'Well, don't worry, Hamal. We'll show you what to do.'

The boy smiled gratefully. He was short and skinny and looked younger than us.

'How old are you?' I asked, as we walked towards the back of the mosque.

'I'm almost eleven,' he whispered.

Farqad and I exchanged disbelieving glances. I dwarfed him, even though I was only just ten. I asked him what year he was in at school and was stunned when he said he was a full school year ahead of me. He was skinny and sickly-looking, as though he had something awful wrong with him. His skin was translucent, paper-thin and pale, and his arms and legs were so scrawny that they looked like matchsticks poking out of his clothes. His big brown eyes were deep-set and surrounded by dark circles of skin, as if he hadn't slept for weeks. He was a sad-looking boy. He may have been almost eleven years old but in my opinion he could have passed for seven.

'Just do as we do,' I told him, 'but don't talk during prayers because it'll make the imam angry.'

Hamal nodded and took his place alongside the boys on the bench opposite us.

As we chatted later, I found out that Hamal lived close to me, in a different part of town from the other children who came on the mosque bus. His parents had just moved to the area and so he had very few friends. I made it my business to become his new best friend at the mosque, because I had an idea that it could be very useful to me.

'Why don't we walk home together?' I suggested. 'Then I won't have to wait for my brother. He's always late.'

Hamal explained that his mother would be picking him up later that night, but he was sure she wouldn't mind me tagging along.

As I fastened the straps of my shoes, I noticed the imam watching me. His eyes followed me as I walked out the mosque door with Hamal and his mother, and he didn't look very happy. Of course, with Hamal living so close by it meant that I wouldn't have to walk alone to the mosque and then wait for Habib to pick me up afterwards. If we arrived and left together there would be no more secret readings in the imam's bedroom. Hamal was the answer to my prayers!

'I'll call for Hamal next time if you like?' I offered, turning to his mother.

'Where do you live?' she asked.

'Just along the road, down there,' I said, pointing to the cluster of houses further along the same street. From Hamal's front garden you could just about make out my house in the distance.

'Okay,' his mother agreed. 'It would be nice for him to have company.'

Hamal smiled at me and I was exhilarated. My lonely walks to the mosque were to become a thing of the past. After all this time, I couldn't believe how easy it was to get away from the stinky imam and our horrible secrets.

Each week night I'd drop into Hamal's house and we would walk the rest of the way to the mosque together. Sometimes his mum would bring his baby sister out in her pram and stroll with us for a bit to get some fresh air. Every night after lessons Hamal and I walked home again, chatting about school and everyday things, and my heart felt light as a bird. He didn't know it, but my sickly little friend had become my personal bodyguard.

Hamal had a great sense of humour and we'd laugh and joke as we walked along. I discovered he hated his shoes as much as I hated mine. Like mine, his were ugly and brown and they were a size too big for his feet, slopping off his heel with every step he took.

'Look,' he said, lifting his trouser leg up to show me. 'I have to wear two pairs of socks just to try and keep them on. I look stupid – like a clown with big long shoes!'

'Hey, don't moan,' I giggled. 'They're not as bad as these!' I offered up my own foot.

Hamal studied it for a moment and nodded his head in agreement. 'You're right, they *are* pretty horrible. I'll show you how to scrape them so badly that your mum will have to buy you new ones.' He ran over to the kerbside and began to grind the leather against the edge of the pavement, roughing it up until it peeled away from the shoe.

'Wow!' I exclaimed. The damage was pretty impressive. His method worked much better than my habit of dragging my toes along the pavement. 'Let me have a go!' I said. The more I scraped at the ugly brown leather, the more we laughed.

I loved walking to mosque with Hamal. It made me feel light-hearted and free. Habib was delighted that he didn't have to pick me up any more, because it meant he could spend more time with his college girlfriend. Everyone was happy. As long as I was with Hamal the imam couldn't hurt me.

I became more confident and cheerful. Even Mum commented on the fact that I seemed brighter.

'Someone's in a good mood today,' she smiled, when she heard me singing along to a Kylie song on the radio. Kylie was my favourite.

The weeks went by until it was a month since the imam had touched me, and I began to feel like a normal person again. I stopped wetting the bed every night; accidents dwindled to only once or twice a week. The sores on my face healed. I felt more outgoing. Things just fell into place.

Hamal was a kind and gentle boy, and I liked him. 'I'm glad we're friends,' I told him, as we walked to the mosque.

'So am I,' he replied.

But the imam was far from happy about our new arrangement, and he decided to make life as difficult as possible for poor little Hamal.

'You stupid boy!' he shouted at him out of the blue one evening, and slapped him around the back of the head.

Hamal was astonished. He'd done absolutely nothing wrong.

'You were talking,' the imam scolded.

It was a lie. Hamal didn't know any of the boys well enough to chat to them. He lowered his head and bit his trembling bottom lip. He was as frightened of the imam as everyone else and didn't dare argue back.

'Sorry,' he said, apologising for something he hadn't even done.

The imam grunted and walked away. Moments later he spun around to face the rest of the children. As he did so, he shot me a look of disgust.

'You must all work harder!' he bellowed.

He seemed to be in a really bad mood.

'I didn't do anything,' Hamal protested on the way home, 'yet he still slapped me. I don't think he likes me very much.'

'Don't be daft. He's just a horrible, angry old man. He hates everyone, even himself!'

Hamal smiled weakly and shrugged, before turning into his driveway. 'See you tomorrow?' he asked.

'See you tomorrow,' I agreed, and carried on towards home.

It turned out that our mothers had a mutual friend and one day we were all invited to her house, where the women could drink tea and chat while the children played. I came running into the kitchen with Hamal, and Mum realised he was the one I was walking to and from the mosque with.

'So this is Hamal,' she said, looking him up and down. She seemed surprised at his skinny, sickly appearance. I think she had been expecting a strapping young lad.

The two women sat down and began to chat.

'Your Nabila's been looking after Hamal for me,' his mother explained.

Mum smiled at me approvingly. 'She's a very kind girl. How's he getting on at the mosque?'

Hamal's mother grimaced. 'He says the imam is very strict.'

'Ahh yes, he is,' Mum replied, 'but then, children need discipline. Don't you agree?'

Hamal and I exchanged horrified glances. We both knew that the imam wasn't just strict; he could be extremely violent, brutal even. Every night, someone would get slapped, and he always hit hard. It was meant to act as a warning to the rest of us to behave, and it worked.

Our mums became firm friends and we were often invited round to their house for a cup of tea. Hamal and I would play in the garden whilst the mums sat inside gossiping. I loved playing with Hamal's baby sister. She was so small and beautiful that it was like having my very own living doll. She'd giggle as I held out toys for her. Hamal and I encouraged her to try and learn to walk, but more often than not she'd collapse on the floor before getting up and trying again. She was certainly determined.

I felt safe and happier than I had in years, but there was one cloud on the horizon. The months since Hamal started coming to the mosque had been blissful for me, but not for him. It was clear to everyone that the imam had it in for him.

'He seems so angry with me the whole time,' Hamal complained, 'but I don't know what I've done wrong. I've had enough.'

My heart froze. I was terrified that he'd leave me but at the same time I felt guilty because I sensed it was my fault the imam picked on him. He couldn't leave; I wouldn't let him. Instead, I tried my best to comfort him.

'The imam picks on everyone, Hamal, not just you. It feels like you're the only one but you're not.'

He grew to hate going to the mosque and would drag his feet all the way there, which meant we'd arrive at five o'clock, just as the other kids were getting off the bus. As soon as we stepped through the mosque door, Hamal knew the next couple of hours were going to be torment.

It had been months since the imam had laid his grubby hands on me – months of freedom, months of happiness. But poor Hamal bore the brunt of my new-found freedom. I'd been his protector to begin with and now he'd become mine, taking beating after beating because of his relationship with me. I knew exactly what was going on. The imam would slap, scold and push poor Hamal around because of his frustration at being unable to do dirty sex things with me any more. The other children wondered out loud what this gentle little boy had done to anger him so much. No one could understand it, except me.

Hamal wasn't the brightest lad in the bunch, but he wasn't stupid either. However, little by little the imam's constant criticism chipped away what little self-confidence he had until he became a quivering wreck.

'You've said your prayers wrong. Do them again!' the imam shouted at him, over and over again.

After a while Hamal became a nervous wreck, and when he was called to read he would stand trembling before the imam, stuttering and stumbling over his

words. Even if he knew the right answer to a question
he'd still manage to say it backwards or pronounce it
incorrectly.

'Stupid boy! Were you born thick or have you just
turned out that way?' the imam would sneer.

He enjoyed bullying my friend and belittling him in
front of everyone else. No one dared to stand up to the
imam, or the slaps and pushes would be directed at
them.

One night he beat Hamal particularly badly.

'If you don't learn your prayers then this is what
you'll get,' he said, swiping him viciously across the face
with the back of his hand. The blow knocked Hamal
backwards and he hit his head hard as he landed on the
floor.

'Get up!' the imam shouted, and he took another
swipe.

Hamal was so skinny that even the slightest slap
would send him flying across the room. He was an easy
target, a sitting duck. Afterwards, the tears pooled in
the corners of my friend's eyes.

'What's this?' the imam jeered. 'Tears on a boy! You
need to be a man!' he mocked, his voice booming across
the hall. He wanted everyone to laugh at Hamal, but no
one did. It wasn't funny.

'You're crying like a little girl. Shall I make you sit
with the girls?' he teased, poking Hamal hard in the
ribs. 'You're as skinny as a girl!'

Hamal sat there with his head bowed and his eyes
down. He didn't know why this man was being so horrible to him. Only the imam and I knew the real reason.

In a bid to cheer Hamal up, I devised some different routes to the mosque. One evening I discovered a way into a huge graveyard and we wandered around looking at all the interesting headstones and strolling among the dead.

'Isn't it weird that all these people walked where we are walking, only hundreds of years ago?' I remarked, as if I was an expert giving a guided tour.

Right from the start, the graveyard made me feel safe. I was never afraid of ghosts, never found it spooky. Looking back, I suppose it's because I knew I'd be protected there. The dead can't hurt you the way the living can.

With the constant beatings he was taking, I lived in fear that Hamal would stop going to the mosque altogether and that the abuse would start all over again. I knew he dreaded going there every night and was tempted to stay in the graveyard and not turn up for lessons, but he would never dare to. He was afraid his parents would find out, and he'd have been forced to go the following night and things would have been even worse for him. Like me, he was trapped.

A few months after Hamal arrived, there was another newcomer: a little eight-year-old girl called Wafa. She was very pretty, with long, dark, poker-straight hair, so shiny that it shone through her thin silk headscarf, and cute little dimples, which revealed themselves whenever she smiled. She was petite for her age and her mother dressed her in a very girly way which made her stand out, just as mine had done. The other girls wore scarves with dull, dark colours, but Wafa had lots of brightly coloured ones and she wore sparkly hairclips. She was different, like a little ray of sunshine. She bloomed against the backdrop of the plain wallflower girls at the mosque.

Wafa was still very young so she arrived holding her mother's hand. You could tell from the way they were dressed that the family was wealthy.

I decided that as she was on her own I'd take Wafa under my wing. I didn't want the other girls picking on her because she was good-looking. I beckoned her over to where Farqad and I were sitting and we began helping her to learn her prayers.

Before long, my mum and dad became friends with Wafa's parents and I was invited round to her house to play. I'd been right about the family being wealthy. Wafa had a mountain of toys and dolls, more than I'd ever dreamed of. I loved going to play at her house. My life was getting better and better, and my confidence was growing. The only bad thing was the two hours at the mosque, with the imam glaring at me, but now that I didn't have the trauma of being taken upstairs I was able to buckle down to my lessons and my work was improving. With any luck, I should have completed the Koran in another year.

One night it was raining, so Hamal and I didn't dawdle and arrived a little earlier than normal. The mosque bus was late and we were still waiting for the other children to turn up. Wafa's mum dropped her off and she came over to stand with us. The imam was downstairs and we could tell that he was in a foul mood because he was slamming books around impatiently, as if he was looking for something he'd lost.

Hamal, Wafa and I were talking quietly when suddenly the imam came storming over.

'Be quiet!' he screamed, his arm raised to hit Hamal.

Hamal curled his hands over his head to protect himself.

'Don't touch him!' I shouted, thrusting my arm out to stop him. The words came from nowhere and took me quite by surprise. I'd had enough of the imam and his bullying ways. I couldn't stand it any longer. I couldn't stand by and watch him attack Hamal yet again.

The imam stopped and glared at me. Hamal was by my side but poor frightened little Wafa was cowering behind us, simply terrified.

'Please don't hurt Hamal any more,' I pleaded, my voice starting to falter. 'I'll help him learn his prayers. I'll help him get better, I promise.'

I waited for the imam to hit me but he didn't. He looked stunned at my intervention, but he thought for a moment and then spoke. 'I won't hit him as long as he learns his prayers.'

'He will,' I promised. 'I'll help him learn them all.'

The imam sucked at his teeth. 'Very well then.' He turned on his heel and walked away.

Hamal peeked nervously through his fingers to check the coast was clear. He could barely believe that he'd escaped this time. Beatings were routine for him now, a part of his life. I could barely believe it myself. For the first time, I'd stood up to the imam.

'Thank you!' Hamal whispered.

Soon we heard the noise of the bus screeching to a halt outside. Within seconds the hall was full of children, all lining up to shake the imam's hand. I glanced at him, trying to read his face. His mood had changed and now he seemed almost happy. I breathed a sigh of relief. My intervention had worked.

We all sat down and began to study our prayer books as usual, watched by the imam. Suddenly, he pointed at Hamal.

'You, boy. Come here!'

My heart sank. What now?

Hamal stumbled to his feet, dropping his prayer book. The imam sighed loudly and rolled his eyes as he waited impatiently in the centre of the room.

I felt an urgent stabbing pain in my chest. It was sheer panic. I watched as Hamal picked up his prayer book and went over to the imam. All eyes were on him.

I waited for the imam to shout and scream at him as usual, but he didn't. Instead, he looked over at me and Wafa, and back at Hamal, then he drew back his fist and punched him really hard in the stomach. The force of the blow knocked him clean off his feet. His skinny legs buckled as he flew several feet through the air before collapsing in a heap on the floor. I held my breath as he lay there, motionless. I thought he might be dead. He was so little, and the imam had hit him with the full force of a grown man's punch.

After a few moments, Hamal began to move. He moaned and whimpered like a wounded animal, then struggled to pull himself to his feet. I could tell he was badly hurt because he was wincing and clutching at his side, and it was only with great difficulty that he hauled himself up and staggered back towards us. He sat down in his place, then suddenly he burst into tears. He sobbed so hard that I thought my heart would break right there and then. I wanted to go over and wrap my arms around him but I daren't. No one wanted to risk being hit by the imam themselves, but the sound of Hamal's crying was awful.

I looked at the imam in horror and he was staring back at me with a look in his eyes that said, '*You don't tell me what to do.*' At that moment I realised that by standing up to him I'd made things a hundred times worse for my friend. It was my fault he'd been punched.

As soon as we got outside the mosque after prayers, I asked Hamal if he was OK. He didn't answer, though. I don't think he could. He was clutching his ribs and staggering, wincing in pain with every step, and it took all his concentration to put one foot in front of the other. There was nothing I could do but walk silently by his side. I felt awful. It seemed to take ages before we got to his driveway and he turned off without a word.

After that, Hamal never came back to the mosque again. I still went round to his house occasionally but we never mentioned the mosque or the imam. I don't know if Hamal's mother ever discussed it with my mum, but, if she did, it didn't make any difference because Mum didn't stop me from going. Maybe she believed I wouldn't get beaten because I was a girl.

All I knew was that without Hamal I was all alone once more.

Chapter 15

Washing Away My Shame

'I've got a special job for you,' the imam told me as lessons finished. 'Wait behind and I'll explain.'

I froze to the spot. It had been months since he'd touched me, but now, with Hamal gone, I knew I was once more at his mercy. Mum hadn't suggested that Habib should start picking me up again – I suppose she reckoned I was old enough to make my own way home – so I planned to slip away as quickly as I could after the last prayer. But there was no way I could run off once the imam had asked me directly to stay behind.

I flinched as he reached out and gripped the top of my arm. My body began to tremble in a way it hadn't for months. I couldn't believe it; it was going to start all over again.

The other children filed out and for the first time in ages we were alone together. He led me towards the entrance of the mosque and pointed at a tin of paint, with two paintbrushes perched on the lid.

'Here,' he said, handing me a brush, 'take this. You can help me paint the inside of the door.'

I looked out through the door and thought about running off down the street. But I knew that even if I did he'd still be waiting for me the following night. His tone was light and friendly but I was all too well aware what he was capable of. There had to be a catch. Nothing was ever straightforward with him.

He handed me a brush and opened the tin of white paint. 'That bit there needs doing,' he said, pointing at a patch where the paint had flaked off, leaving bare wood exposed, and he started on a higher-up bit himself.

I tried to stop myself trembling. He couldn't touch me if we were simply painting a door side by side. There might be passers-by in the street just a few feet away. Anyone could walk in. Still, it felt horrible to be alone with him, so close that I could smell the horrible odours of his breath, his armpits, his skin.

The patch he wanted me to paint was low down so I squatted on my heels. He was standing very close, right behind me. I hadn't done much painting before and was worried I'd make a mess of it.

I tried to calm myself. He couldn't touch me if we were just painting. Still, my body shook with fear. I was trapped here alone with him. My heart raced as adrenaline pumped around my body at breakneck speed.

'This bit needs doing,' he said, pointing to a patch on the wood directly beneath him. I gulped and nodded obediently. My hands were shaking as I wriggled between him and the door and crouched down into a squatting position. I tried my best to paint but the angle was all wrong and I couldn't reach part of it. He was standing over me, painting a patch higher up, and I was hemmed in. Panic rose within me. I wanted to finish as soon as I could so I didn't have to stay a moment longer than necessary.

The imam looked down and sighed. 'That's not working, is it?' He dragged over a nearby chair. 'Here, I'll sit down and you can paint the bottom bit of the door while sitting on my lap.'

My mouth went bone dry and I felt sick but I had no choice but to obey. As soon as I sat on his lap, the imam began to paw at my body with his free hand. He was painting with his right hand and stroking me with his left.

'*If I ignore him, maybe he'll stop,*' I prayed in my head.

But he didn't. I felt the familiar itch of his white beard against my neck and his hot breath on my cheek. The scent of his rotten teeth filled my nostrils. Then his lips were on my face and he was biting and sucking at my cheeks. My eyes smarted with tears. I could feel a bruise forming as he sucked and bit me, sinking his teeth into me like an animal. It felt as if he was feeding on me, tearing at my flesh, eating me piece by piece until there was nothing left.

I squirmed in his arms as his free hand ran up and down my body, over my clothes, and then slid under the top of my trousers and down into my pants. I thought of his dirty fingernails as he pushed his fingers hard inside me. I wanted to scream out, to run. I wanted him to stop. I wanted him to die. *I* wanted to die. If I was dead he wouldn't be able to hurt me any more.

'I've missed you,' he whispered, moving his fingers in and out of my body, rubbing me raw.

I was scared that he'd drip white gloss paint all over my clothes. My mum would see it and guess what I'd been up to. I was certain she'd be able to smell him on me. Everyone would see the paint and somehow they'd know about my shame.

I shut my eyes and tried to block him out but the smell of his body odour lingered in the air. His foul stench was all over me. I would have to scrub myself clean afterwards. His hands were on me, making me dirtier and dirtier. He was whispering and moaning in my ear. Suddenly I felt the hard thing in his pants. He put his paintbrush down on the pot, lifted his sarong and reached into his pants.

'I've got to go!' I gasped, dropping the brush in horror. It fell to the floor, spraying white paint all around it. I had paint on my hands and I panicked. How would I hide it from Mum? I had to wash myself before she saw me. He'd made me dirty and now the paint had marked me as well. I needed to scour myself clean, but I couldn't do it in the mosque. I had to get out. I had to run.

The imam laughed at my distress and said, 'Calm down, Nabila. What's up with you?'

I hated him. I hated him for doing this to me. As I grabbed at the door, my fingers stuck to it. I opened it just enough to squeeze through and sprinted off into the night. I ran all the way down the road and didn't stop

running until I could see the lights of our house. I
hurried straight up to the bathroom, where I locked the
door. I needed to scrub myself to get the paint and the
scent of the imam off my skin. I ran a deep bath, as hot
as I could make it, tied my hair up in a bun on top of
my head, and sighed as I slid into the water and let it
flow over me.

'Aren't you coming for dinner, Nabila?' Mum
shouted.

'I'll be down soon,' I called. She didn't ask why I was
having a bath, too busy with preparing the meal.

I was filled with despair. It had started again and
there was nothing I could do. He would always find a
way to be alone with me. There was no escape and,
once I was with him, I had no choice but to do as he
told me.

The following night, after lessons finished, the imam
was waiting for me again.

'Come upstairs, Nabila,' he commanded.

'I have to get home,' I said.

'I need you to do something for me. Come along
now.'

I watched the other children filing out to the bus,
willing them to look round and see my distress, to
somehow save me, but they were talking among themselves, caught up in their own worlds. Farqad gave me
a wave, as did Wafa, but neither noticed that I was
upset. When they'd gone, the imam took my arm and
pushed me in front of him up the stairs. We went into
the office, sat at the desk and he put his hand straight
inside his pants, the way he'd started to do the night

before. I looked away in embarrassment and stared at the pattern in the wallpaper.

Despite living in a house with four brothers, I'd never seen a man's willy before. I'd heard girls talk about them in the playground and I knew boys liked playing with them but I had no idea what they looked like. I glanced down for a moment and was shocked at the ugly red thing he was holding, and the way he was moving his hand up and down it. It was horrible. What was he doing? I didn't want to watch but he just carried on in front of me.

'Don't worry,' he said, reaching out a hand to catch hold of my arm. I reeled backwards in horror. I didn't want him touching me with his hand after he'd just touched himself down there.

'Men do this all the time,' he chuckled. 'Come closer, Nabila.'

But I was frozen. There was no way I was going near that thing, or near him. I was terrified of what he'd do to me. Suddenly, I felt a warm trickle down the inside of my leg. I looked down in horror and realised there was a dark patch on the front of my trousers. I'd wet myself. I was mortified, humiliated. I was supposed to be a big girl but here I was, wetting myself like a baby. The wee had stained the fabric, giving away my secret for all to see. I looked at the imam but he was still busy playing with himself. I hated him. He'd made me do that – he'd made me wet myself in fear.

Just then he grunted and some white stuff oozed out of his willy and onto his hand. His face contorted and at first I thought he was in pain. What had he done to himself? Was he injured? I must have looked astonished because the imam laughed as he wiped his hands on his sarong.

'Have you never seen that before? It's a natural thing. Now I need you to come upstairs to the third floor with me.'

'I don't want to,' I whispered, my voice shaking. I'd never been up to that floor before.

'OK, stay here for now, but you have to come up when I call for you.'

As I stood, my heart thumping in my chest, I considered making a run for it, but I was too scared. He had absolute power over me and he knew it.

Moments later, he shouted down my name. As I climbed the stairs with legs like lead I felt sure I was going to faint. My mind was whirring, worrying frantically about what he was going to do next. Would he make me touch his willy? I didn't want to get that white stuff on me. Would he put his finger inside me and hurt me again?

'Nabila!' he called angrily. I dashed the rest of the way because I didn't want to get into any trouble.

On the third floor landing I saw a wooden door that was slightly ajar, and I could hear the sound of water splashing inside. I pushed the door and peeped round the edge to find the imam sitting stark naked in an old-fashioned tin bath. He had soaped his back and was holding out a cup.

'Help me rinse off,' he ordered.

I shook my head and cowered behind the door. He looked even uglier than usual with no clothes on, his belly sticking out in a big round circle and his willy floating in the water. He beckoned me to come over. It was disgusting. Awful. I couldn't bear it.

Suddenly I turned and ran downstairs as fast as I could and, as I went, I heard him calling after me: 'See you tomorrow then.' He gave a chuckle and I couldn't understand what was funny. He must know this was a terrible thing to do, to let a young girl see you in the bath. He didn't care. He was evil.

When I got home that evening, I couldn't bring myself to give my dad a hug goodnight. From that moment on I looked at him and my brothers differently. Did they play with their willies just as the imam did? Was that what boys and men did? Was it something they did on their own or with girls? I knew Dad would never harm me but the thought that he might do those things himself made me want to throw up.

Later that night I wet the bed for the first time in ages. I thought I'd grown out of it but it had come back to haunt me, along with terrifying nightmares in which the imam was naked and beckoning to me. I couldn't escape him. Even in my sleep he was always there. The following morning I climbed out of my sodden bed and the familiar stench of stale wee filled the air. It was back to the old routine of flipping the mattress and turning the sheet round so Mum wouldn't find out.

I ran to the bathroom and washed myself in ice-cold water. I didn't want to risk using up all the hot water because I knew Dad liked to have a bath in the morning. The cold water was good. It shocked me and reminded me that I was unclean.

I needed to be punished for being such a dirty girl.

Chapter 16

The
Protector

The abuse had started all over again and I thought about it constantly. Sometimes I watched Mum cooking in the kitchen and sat there practising in my head the words I'd use to tell her about the imam and what he was doing to me when we were alone. But every time I opened my mouth to speak, the words refused to come out. Instead, they'd stay there, lodged in my throat like a brick.

Mum was always stressed and tired, so there was never a good moment. She had her hands full looking after all of us and running the house, so we never sat down for a chat. She never asked me how my life was. If she had, maybe I'd have been able to say 'I hate it' and then she would have forced the story out of me. But our only communications seemed to be when she was telling me off for something. She was always in a bad mood. Whenever I thought about telling her about the imam pawing my body and doing strange things to his own willy, I imagined the shock on her face, and I knew she would be furious with me, not him. Things would get ten times worse for me.

'Why are you hanging around, Nabila?' she nagged every night. 'If you've finished your tea, get off to the mosque.' I grabbed my coat, shut the door and headed for the mosque, sent by my own mother into the hands of the man who was abusing me.

When I got there, the imam was always waiting. If it was early and there was time before the other children arrived, he made me follow him upstairs and as he sat me on his lap I could feel his thing sticking into me through my clothes. He would run his hands all over my body and soon his fingers would be inside me.

'*Be brave*,' I told myself. I imagined that I was a soldier and that I had to go through this to save other little children. If he did this to me, then he wouldn't touch the others. I would suffer so that they didn't have to.

I tried not to cry out. I tried to be strong because I didn't want the imam to know how much I was suffering. That way he would have won. Maybe if I obeyed, it wouldn't get any worse. Maybe I'd never have to touch him back. That's what I thought – but I was wrong.

'Here,' he gasped one night, shoving me abruptly from his lap. He lifted the hem of his grubby sarong and pulled his willy out of his pants.

'Touch it,' he demanded. 'Touch it now!'

He was shouting. From his tone of voice I knew he wouldn't take no for an answer. There was nowhere left to run or hide. I had to do this.

He grabbed my hands and I shut my eyes as he placed them against his willy, which felt hot and horrid. He wrapped my fingers around it and held them so that I couldn't let go then began to move them up and down.

'Faster, faster!' he gasped.

Eventually, just as my arms were beginning to burn, I felt something warm and wet all on my fingers. It was the white stuff and it was all over me.

'Don't worry,' he said, as I looked down in horror at the mess on my hands. 'It's normal. It's what happens.'

He passed me some tissues with which to wipe myself. When I looked at his face he was smiling and seemed very pleased with himself. I held my hands away from me, feeling the slimy stuff between my fingers and worried it would get on my clothes. It was bad enough having him touch me, but this was worse. I felt dirty both inside and out. I ran to the bathroom and rinsed my hands under the tap, then suddenly my stomach clenched and I threw up into the toilet. I picked up the grimy bar of soap off the edge of the sink and used it to scrub my hands, legs and body, trying to wash every trace of him from my skin.

As soon as I got home I started running a hot bath. Mum heard the tap and followed me into the bathroom, making me jump. I'd become so jumpy that I was even frightened of my own shadow.

'Do you want me to help you wash your hair?' she asked.

'No, I'm fine. I can do it myself.'

'Well, just be sure to rinse it out properly.'

I locked the door, took off my clothes and allowed my body to sink deep into the hot clean water. The soap felt creamy and lovely as I washed myself thoroughly from my toes upwards. I couldn't leave a single bit untouched – his hands had been all over me. Using my fingernails, I scrubbed and scratched at my skin, but still I didn't feel clean enough. I needed something stronger.

Moments later Asif was hammering at the door. 'Are you going to be much longer? I'm dying for a piss!'

'Won't be long …' I lied.

I grabbed a little mirror and studied myself. I hated my face: it was what had got me into all this trouble in the first place. Why couldn't I just be plain and ugly, then the imam wouldn't like me any more? I had a fresh love bite on my cheek that I would have to conceal somehow. What was it about my cheeks that made him want to bite them all the time? I couldn't understand it. I pinched and scratched at them, trying to stop myself being pretty. I'd have done anything to stop the imam wanting me.

'I had to have a piss out in the garden thanks to you!' Asif hissed as I eventually padded to my bedroom wrapped in a big towel.

I slammed the bedroom door shut. Everyone hated me. Everyone thought I was stupid and smelly. I didn't want to be Nabila any more. I wanted to be someone else. I wanted to be somewhere else.

In the bedroom mirror I looked at my body, which was filling out more every day. I had rounded breasts and hips, and little wisps of hair were beginning to appear around my private parts. I hated all these changes. Mum still hadn't talked to me about sex or periods or where babies came from, but one day she gave me a tube of hair removal cream.

'You need to use this on your private parts when the hair comes,' she told me. 'Muslim women should be hairless down below. Just follow the instructions on the tube.'

That was the extent of the guidance she gave me. I hated the smell of that cream but I smeared it all over myself and waited five minutes, then when I wiped it off the hair came too.

I dreaded everything about growing up. The white girls at school looked forward to wearing their first bra and their periods starting, but to me they sounded horrid. I didn't realise that perhaps growing up might be a good thing. Perhaps it would eventually make the imam go off me because his taste was for younger, less mature girls. For the time being, the abuse was relentless, and I was completely in his power.

'As soon as you arrive in the evening, come straight upstairs so we can do our reading,' he said.

The word 'reading' sounded innocuous but really it meant 'abuse'. He began to play with himself regularly in front of me and to ask me to hold his willy – 'pleasuring him', he called it. I didn't understand the way he used the word 'pleasure' because I felt no pleasure in what he was doing, only fear.

'This is nice,' he whispered in Urdu. 'Isn't it nice?'

I never said anything.

A few weeks later, I arrived at the mosque and headed straight up to the imam's room, just as I'd been told to. I guessed he'd be waiting for me and, in a way, I wanted to get it over and done with. My mind was full of dread about what he would do to me that evening, but the sooner I went up there, the sooner it would be over, and at least if I 'pleasured' him before lessons began then I could run straight home afterwards and jump into the bath. I was so lost in my own thoughts that I didn't hear the muffled voices coming from inside his room. I pushed open the heavy door and stepped in.

In the half-light I could see the imam's outline where he sat in his usual chair, but there was someone else with him. I blinked as my eyes adjusted to the gloom, then gasped when I made out the outline of a little girl. She was standing in front of him, between his knees, and one of his hands was clamped round her waist while another was stroking her head and back.

At that moment, a floorboard creaked under my foot and both heads spun around to look at me. The imam was startled and cross. The little girl's eyes were wide with fright and I reeled in horror when I realised it was Wafa. Pure hatred filled my body. He'd ruined me and now he'd started on someone new. He was about to ruin another young life, as if mine wasn't enough.

Suddenly, the room felt as if it was closing in. Wafa was so tiny, innocent, precious and pure. It was hideous to think of him touching her. At least he didn't have his willy out, but still, I couldn't bear to see his hands on her. I held out my arms and she broke free from the imam's grasp and ran over to where I was standing. Her fingers trembled as she clutched my hand tightly in hers and huddled against me.

I looked up at the imam defiantly. There were two of us and we were united against him. He seemed surprised at first, then he gave me a look of pure and utter disgust and snorted loudly. He was challenging me to defy him. He didn't think I had it in me.

'Don't touch her,' I begged. 'Don't do it to her. Please. Do whatever you want to me, just leave her alone!'

Wafa slipped round to hide behind me.

The imam laughed. 'You don't know what you are talking about. You're just silly little girls.'

'Do it to me, not to her. Leave her alone,' I repeated, more forcefully than before.

My hands were shaking. I didn't have a clue what he'd do next but, whatever it was, I knew for sure I wouldn't let him touch her. I couldn't let him ruin another young life.

Wafa clung to me like a limpet, her face buried deep into my side. I hoped things hadn't gone too far already. When he first brought me up to that room, he used to put his hand round my waist and stroke my head and back, just as I'd seen him do to her. I hoped I'd caught him in time and that it hadn't gone any further. Already she had experienced something that no child should ever have to go through.

Suddenly, the imam spoke, breaking the silence: 'Go downstairs – both of you.'

I held Wafa's hand tightly as we fled down to the hall below, where we sat on a bench. Neither of us spoke about what had happened. I didn't know what to say to her. She knew my secret because of what I had blurted out in the room upstairs, and I knew something about what had been happening to her as well, but we didn't speak. It was almost as if, by not talking about it, it stopped it all from being real.

I was still holding Wafa's hand when the other children arrived. She brightened up when she saw them, as if she knew that we were safe – there was safety in numbers. Suddenly she piped up and began chatting to me about her doll's tea set. It was a surreal conversation, as if nothing had happened, as if the past ten minutes had just been a dream.

'Would you like to come and play at my house again one day?' she chirped.

'Yes, I'd like that,' I replied.

Thank goodness, it seemed as though I'd caught him in time. I would be able to protect her in a way I'd failed to protect Hamal. He'd been beaten senseless because of me, but now I could do something good – now I could save little Wafa. I wouldn't let the imam do to her what he'd done to me. No way. Wafa was a beautiful little girl and she needed to stay pure. He had soiled me but I wouldn't let him ruin her.

I wondered why he had turned to her. And then it hit me. Maybe it was because I was getting too old for him. Perhaps he liked frightened little girls, not older ones like me who could challenge his behaviour. Maybe he preferred younger girls' bodies to ones with breasts and hips and hair growing around their private parts.

I decided I'd have to make sure I always got to the mosque early and didn't leave till after Wafa's mum had picked her up so that the imam never got a chance to be on his own with her. I also resolved that I would talk to her some time about what he did to me. She was the only one who'd understand; she alone knew what he was capable of.

But after a few more weeks little Wafa never came to the mosque again. No explanation was given and I began to worry that maybe she had told someone about what the imam had done to her. If so, she was bound to have mentioned me. If she remembered what I had said to him about doing it to me, not her, then everyone would find out about my dark, horrible secret.

Now I had a new fear to live with – that one day soon I'd be found out.

Chapter 17

Self-harm and Scourers

With both Hamal and Wafa gone, I felt utterly alone at the mosque. I wished I could stop going, but when I asked my parents they said they wouldn't hear of it until I'd learned the Koran.

I was still good friends with Farqad, but she had no idea what was happening to me in the imam's upstairs room. I wished I could tell her, but how could I? It would be a scandal. My parents would hate me and so would my brothers. Everyone would turn away from me, saying I'd brought shame upon my family, upon the community. The imam was a respected pillar of the Muslim community. People fought amongst each other about whose turn it was to invite him for tea, and they made him a guest of honour at their dinner tables. I was just a silly little girl, so why would anyone believe me? I felt like damaged goods. I was dirty little Nabila – but I had begun to form a plan to get myself clean again.

By the time I was eleven the imam was regularly pleasuring himself with me, his white fluid sticking to the skin of my hands and his saliva covering my face and neck. As soon as I could get away I wanted to scour myself clean to get every last trace of him off me, but soap and water didn't seem enough.

One day, I watched Mum washing pots in the kitchen sink. She used a scouring pad to scrub vigorously at the bottoms of the stainless steel pans. Not only did the scourer remove all stubborn traces of food, but it also made the pans shiny and clean again. They gleamed brightly on the draining board as if they were brand new. I decided I needed to make myself just like those pans.

Later that day, when Mum wasn't looking, I sneaked into the kitchen and snatched one of the new scourers from a packet in the cupboard under the sink. There were dozens of them so I knew she'd never notice one missing. I pushed it deep into my cardigan pocket and disappeared up into my bedroom, shutting the door.

I held the scourer in my hands. It was round in shape and made of shiny, wiry plastic, and when I brushed it against my arm it felt rough against my skin, as though it had hidden teeth. It was perfect.

That night, after getting in from the mosque, I went straight to my bedroom for the scourer, then locked myself in the bathroom. Moments later there was a knock at the door – it was Mum.

'Nabila, is that you? Don't use all the hot water because your father might want a bath later on. Understand?'

'Yes.' I sighed as I turned the hot tap on full and poured bubble bath under the jet. I loved that moment when I could immerse my naked body in the hot water, letting it wash over my skin, but I couldn't rest that night – I had work to do.

I lathered the bar of soap between my fingers, then rubbed the scourer furiously against the soap. It scratched away at the surface, like a knife against butter. This would make me nice and clean.

I started with my feet. The plastic felt scratchy against the delicate skin of my toes and soon they were stinging where I'd rubbed. I dipped them back under the hot water and my skin smarted satisfactorily. I moved up to my legs and then my bum and belly. I brushed briskly at my skin, moving the soap-filled scourer straight across the surface, like a wood plane shaving away dead wood. Again, my body stung when I dipped it back under the hot water, but I liked the pain – it made me feel better.

I scrubbed at my breasts, under my armpits and then I opened my legs and ran the scourer around my private parts. It hurt badly when I scrubbed there, but I had to do it – I had to get the smell of the imam off me. The more I scoured, the more it stung, but when I had finished I went back and scoured myself once more from the toes up, just in case I had missed a bit. I scoured parts where he didn't touch me as well, just to be on the safe side.

Soon I was scrubbing my skin like this four, even five times a week. My body was dry and red raw and patches of skin began to bleed where I had rubbed too hard. I dabbed the bleeding bits with handfuls of toilet paper, trying to stem the flow of blood, but still I scoured myself.

When the first scourer had almost worn out, I stole a second one. This time it was yellow, the colour of sunshine, but just like the last one it scratched my skin red raw. The pain kept me awake at night.

Once I'd been frightened of witches in the wallpaper, but now I was frightened of the imam's germs on my skin. I washed my hands over and over again until the skin between my fingers became dry and cracked. It peeled and flaked away, but that was good because it meant I was growing a new skin – a whole new me. The more my skin peeled, the better I felt. The old infected layers were coming off and a brand new skin was coming through underneath. But every time I grew another layer, the imam would taint it and I'd have to wash and try to strip it away all over again. The washing became relentless.

I would wake early in the mornings in a wet bed, the urine stinging at my scoured-raw skin like acid. It burnt in deep as I dashed to the bathroom to start the washing process all over again. I was exhausted by it all.

Meanwhile, the abuse continued several times a week, week in, week out.

One night I simply couldn't face it. When the school bell rang, the usual feeling of dread overwhelmed me and panic gripped my stomach. Not again. I couldn't go there, not tonight. I took the decision that I wouldn't go. I'd skip one night. Maybe I could pretend to Mum I was sick. I shook the thought from my head

– she would never believe me. I'd been at school all day and if I was well enough for that then as far as she was concerned I was well enough to go to the mosque. I had to think of something else. I wouldn't go to the mosque tonight, but where on earth could I go instead?

The answer came to me on my way there. As I took my shortcut through the graveyard, I decided that I would stay and wander amongst the dead a little longer. I'd be safe with them – they couldn't hurt me. I passed the next two and a half hours wandering around the graveyard, looking at all the names and ages on the headstones. I was shocked at how young some of the children had been when they died, years and years ago. Some were even younger than me. Part of me wished I could swap places with them. At least if I was cold and dead the imam wouldn't be able to touch me or kiss me any more. The cold earth would protect me. I'd be hiding under the soil where no one could see me.

After that, I regularly started skipping my mosque lessons. Instead, I'd wander around the graveyard, making mental notes of which graves I'd already looked at and which ones I still needed to visit. Sometimes I'd tidy up the flowers on the graves. If one person didn't have any, I'd take them some from another grave where there were lots. I'd share them all out because I wanted them all to feel as loved as the next person.

The graveyard was vast. Lots of people used it as a cut-through to the main road, but no one thought to ask the little girl on the bench what she was doing there all alone at night. What was so unbearable about her life that she felt better sitting amongst the dead and buried bodies rather than being with the living?

After seven o'clock I slowly made my way back home. I knew it was time to leave because I'd been given a new digital watch with a chunky pink strap for my eleventh birthday. I never told anyone about my graveyard visits, and no one ever asked. Mum and Dad presumed I'd been at the mosque. I wondered what they'd do if they found out that I was skiving. They'd be furious, but as long as the imam couldn't get his hands on me, that was all that mattered. I'd still go to the mosque a couple of times a week, because if I'd missed too many nights in a row he would have phoned my parents to ask where I was. It got so that I'd spend one night at the mosque then miss the next two or three. He still made me come up to his room to play his filthy games on the nights when I was there, but I just had to get through it then I could look forward to a couple of nights at the graveyard.

'Why haven't you been coming so often?' Farqad asked.

'I've been sick,' I lied.

She narrowed her eyes and looked down at her prayer book. She didn't believe me, but I couldn't tell her where I'd really been or why.

The imam only asked me once why I'd been absent and I gave the same answer I'd given Farqad. I thought he'd ask me lots of questions but he didn't. Instead, he just grunted and walked off. His reaction made me feel ever braver about skipping lessons.

I was coming towards the end of my studies anyway, so a few missed lessons here and there wouldn't make much difference. I was getting better at timing it so that on the nights when I did go I arrived just as the mosque bus pulled up and I entered the hall with all the other children, then I'd do my best to slip out quickly at the end before he could intercept me. The imam realised what I was doing, though, and positioned himself by the door so he could say, 'Nabila, a moment please. There's something I have to show you.' Then I would have no choice but to wait behind and go upstairs to the dreaded room with him.

On those evenings, as soon as I got home I'd head straight to the bathroom and, while my bath was running, I'd pinch the skin of my face between my fingertips until the pain got too much. When I let go another bruise would be forming. Then I would get into the bath and scour my body with a scouring pad till I was bright red all over. Maybe I was trying to disguise the places where he had touched, kissed and bitten me, to cover his tracks. I don't really know why I damaged myself, but maybe, subconsciously, I wanted someone to notice and do something about it. On a conscious level, of course, I was desperate to keep my secret hidden. Mum nagged at me endlessly to stop harming my face but it never seemed to occur to her to ask why I was doing it. She thought it was simply a bad habit I'd got into.

Friends at school caught me pinching and scratching my face in lessons and thought I was a bit strange – an oddball. I was the girl with bruises on her face even though no one had hit her. I'd done it all to myself. Then I got into the habit of putting my hands over my face to cover up what I'd done. Constantly touching, pulling and pawing my face made the skin greasy. The more I scrubbed at it, the more oil it produced, and soon I started getting spots. One boy, Sab, the son of our old prying shop neighbour Aariz, called me 'Pizza Face' and I hated him for it.

'Hey, watch out! Here comes Pizza Face!' he'd laugh until I wanted to kick him.

One day I opened the bathroom cabinet and saw one of Habib's Bic razors. I took it out and held it in my hand. I twisted it around in my fingers and studied the sharp line of the metal, trapped between the layers of the thin plastic head.

I looked at my face and then back at the razor. Three of my brothers shaved every day. Their dark hair meant that they'd have a five o'clock shadow long before the end of the day. I looked at my own skin. It was smooth, apart from the spots dotted around my chin and nose.

I took the razor and pressed the blade hard against a spot. It immediately burst. I was delighted. I took a piece of tissue and squeezed it until it bled. The blood was crimson red and pooled on the surface before trickling down my chin. It was strange but as soon as I saw the blood I felt better.

I held the razor against another bit of my face that I'd already scratched with my fingernails. I pressed it down, cutting the scratch to make it open up and bleed. The pain was sharp but as soon as it began to bleed I was filled with relief.

I dabbed and cut, dabbed and cut, until my face was a network of tiny cuts. None of them were deep but they left stinging little nicks on the surface. I dabbed them with tissues until the bleeding stopped, put the razor back in the cupboard and pulled my hair across my face so no one in the house would notice.

That night I couldn't sleep. The cuts had felt good somehow, as if the blood had contained the poison that the imam had left behind. If I could get the poison out of me then I'd be clean again. The next morning when I looked in the mirror, though, I was shocked to see the mess I'd made of my face. It looked as though I had been pushed in a thorn bush or showered with tiny fragments of glass. It had given me a feeling of release at the time, but I couldn't go on like this. If Mum didn't notice, one of the teachers at school might. I'd have to find another way to provide relief.

A few nights later I was soaking in the bath. I'd already scoured and washed my body countless times and the water was beginning to grow cold. I kept thinking about the razor in the cabinet, and finally I got out of the bath, grabbed it and stepped back into the water. I didn't even know what I was going to do next. I just knew that everything felt right when I had that razor in my hands.

I lay back down in the water and leant my head against the side of the bathtub, then glanced down along my body. It was a familiar landscape but I hated it. The imam liked to touch and feel my body. He liked it so much that he had made me hate it.

The razor twisted beneath my fingers, catching the light. It glinted back at me, as if it was daring me to do my worst.

I lifted one leg out of the water and gripped a tap with my toes, then I drew the razor across my skin. It sliced down every single hair in its path until my leg was smooth and hairless. It looked new and soft, just like a baby's. I traced my finger up the shaved shin. It felt silky and clean. I twisted my ankle and admired my work. Perfect.

Then I started on the other leg, but the angle was awkward and soon I'd pressed too deep. A long crimson stripe appeared. The colour peeked through at first, like a thin red biro mark, then it got wider and blood began to spill out. The razor had been so sharp that I hadn't felt any pain. I watched in amazement as the blood ran along my leg in a trickle, pooling as it gathered speed, collecting more blood en route and dripping furiously into the bathwater below. The blood hit the surface as pure crimson drops which immediately dispersed, making the water a murky pink.

I don't know why I didn't panic, but somehow the flow and colour of the dripping blood made me feel better. It was as though the badness was draining out of me. I watched with morbid fascination as it drip-dripped into the water. A stinging pain started to set in as the cold air hit the open wound, but I ignored it at first. Pain was good. It made me feel better.

There was a hammering at the door and Dad's voice called, 'How much longer are you going to be in there, Nabila?'

I thrust my leg back down into the water. 'Sorry, Dad, just coming.'

The warmth of the bath drew the blood out even faster until it was gushing all around me. I imagined sharks circling in an open sea; I'd be easy prey with all this blood. By now the rest of the water was taking on a pinky-red hue. I got out of the bath, pulled out the plug and watched as it washed away, swirling down the plughole. The colour looked almost pretty.

I hopped over to the toilet roll and wrapped a huge wad of paper around my hand and held it tight against the cut on my leg. I put the razor away in the cabinet and checked there were no tell-tale smears of blood left in the bath. When the coast was clear in the landing outside, I wrapped a towel round me, pulled my dressing gown on top and limped across to the safety of my bedroom.

It took ages for my leg to stop bleeding and, once it had, I was delighted when I saw a crusty scab growing. I felt as though I'd healed myself.

I already kept my own supply of special scourers hidden in an old wooden box in the bathroom, which was pushed towards the back of the cabinet. No one ever looked inside it, not even Dad. Now I put a razor in there was well, and instantly I felt much better. It meant that I could make myself new and clean again whenever I needed to. In some ways the pain from the cuts made me stronger.

The next time, I drew the blade over the same cut, reopening the old wound. As soon as the crimson stripe appeared I felt better, as if I'd been greeted by an old friend. After that I began making lots of new cuts on my legs. Each one brought me a sense of relief from my ongoing torment at the mosque. With each cut I was taking more and more control over my own body. I began to cut myself even on nights when I hadn't been abused, and during the day at weekends as well. I couldn't fight the strong urge to harm myself. My secret remained hidden underneath my trousers and long knee-high socks.

If I could stand this pain, then I could stand anything. The fear was still there but now there was a new, stronger Nabila fighting to get out. She was tough and she had the scars to prove it. I hoped that this new girl would be strong enough to fight back harder until the abuse finally stopped once and for all.

Chapter 18

Saying 'No'

At the age of eleven, I was cutting myself regularly. I was careful that no one ever saw the damage. If I had to change in front of the other girls for gym class, I'd wrap a towel round myself and pull on my trousers or long socks under cover. It was my secret, something I kept from the rest of the world, and it helped me to cope. Hurting myself made me feel better, almost as if I was taking control of things – but of course I wasn't.

I frequently wet myself, either in bed at night, or sometimes through fear when standing in the mosque as the imam had his way with me. I'd splash myself clean in the toilets there then come home and scrub my body even more vigorously. In the morning I had the same cycle of turning the mattress and sheet, then going to school terrified that someone would smell wee on me. Before all this started I'd been outgoing and happy – the fastest girl in the playground – but now I fretted and worried constantly. I spent more and more time at the graveyard, hiding amongst the headstones, or in the bathroom, hacking at my legs. I scratched and battered my face then pulled my hair loose from its plaits and clasped it self-consciously across my cheeks. Maybe without realising it I was trying to make people notice. Maybe it was a secret cry for help.

At my last parents' evening at primary school my teacher remarked on what a quiet child I'd become.

'Nabila never speaks up in class or puts up her hand to answer questions any more. I'm hoping that she'll come out of her shell a bit more when she goes to secondary school in the autumn.'

Mum shook her head and tutted.

'She's the same at home,' Dad said. 'She used to be more outgoing. I don't know what's wrong with her.'

Afterwards, Mum was exasperated with me: 'Why don't you talk any more?' she demanded. 'You never used to be shy.'

I wanted to blurt out the truth, but the words wouldn't come. I couldn't tell her because it would ruin their lives too.

The teacher wasn't the only one. Our old nosey neighbour Aariz commented that when he visited in the past I used to be the cheeky, pretty one who was always laughing and showing off, but now I'd turned into a quiet little mouse.

It was as though I'd lost my voice and lost my way. I couldn't think what to say to anyone any more. Instead, I'd run to my bedroom and talk to Kylie Minogue. I loved Kylie – I idolised her. I had her posters stuck all over my bedroom wall. *Neighbours*, the Australian TV programme in which she played Charlene, had just moved to a teatime slot and I always tried to catch it before leaving for the mosque. I loved her character, a pretty schoolgirl who became a car mechanic.

'I wish I could be more like you,' I whispered up to her. 'I wish I lived in Australia with you because the imam wouldn't be able to get me.'

Charlene was strong enough to stand up to boys and she would definitely have stood up to the imam if she'd been in my situation. At night, I dreamt of being a bridesmaid at Charlene's wedding to her dishy boyfriend Scott, played by Jason Donovan. I wanted a little bit of their fairytale for myself.

When Kylie was singing one of her pop hits, I'd escape to a different and better world. I wanted to live in Australia. Unlike the Midlands, everyone in Australia seemed so nice and cheerful and it was always sunny on the other side of the world. It was thousands of miles away from here and thousands of miles away from the imam. Instead of practising my prayers, I'd practise Kylie's dance moves around my bedroom. If I could dance like her then maybe I could *be* her and not be me any more.

I really was Kylie's biggest fan. Every Friday when Dad gave me my pocket money, I'd run to the corner shop and buy *Smash Hits* magazine so I could read all about her. I'd record her songs off the radio and wait by it with bated breath to see what number her latest song was in the charts. Kylie was always number one to me. I was so desperate to meet her that I even wrote to the

TV show *Jim'll Fix It* and asked the host, Jimmy Savile, if he could fix it for me to meet Kylie. I never heard back, though.

Dream as I might, I wasn't Kylie: I was Nabila and I was stuck here in rainy England. I had no one to turn to and nowhere else to go. I couldn't escape to Australia; it was just a silly dream.

Around this time, Dad, Tariq and Habib went to Pakistan to visit some relatives, and when Dad and Tariq got back they had some dramatic news for us. Habib had got married to a girl called Fajr and was staying out there with her for a year, then they would be coming back to live with us. It was a very wealthy family and a good match for him. What was more, they were talking about arranging a marriage for me with Fajr's younger brother. As the only boy, he would inherit the family business so I would always be well off if I married him.

I greeted the news with apprehension. I was still only eleven so the wedding would be some years off but I couldn't help wondering what this boy would be like. Then I panicked at the thought of marriage. My future husband would want to have sex with me and I knew I would never be able to do it without thinking of the dirty old imam and all the horrific things he did to me. The thought of having to do these things again was just awful, even if it was with someone my own age who didn't smell of body odour and rotting teeth.

I hoped the marriage would never happen, although Dad said that a promise had been made between the families. I'd always known I'd have an arranged marriage one day but still I couldn't help hankering after the romantic kind of love you saw on the telly. I thought of Kylie, of Charlene, who had dishy Scott, when all I had was the filthy imam. *Was he my boyfriend?* I shuddered. Maybe he was all I deserved. Maybe I'd never have a nice boyfriend; maybe I'd be trapped with the imam forever – or until I married this stranger who was Habib's new brother-in-law.

One night after prayers, when the imam ordered me to come upstairs with him, I looked down at his dirty fingers gripping my arms, smelt the horrible odour of stale spices, stinky armpits and bad breath, and my stomach lurched.

'What's the matter?' he panted as we reached the top of the stairs. 'Don't you like coming up here with me?'

I shook my head in despair but he ignored me, just led me by the hand into the office. I expected him to get out the prayer book and make me read while he groped my body, but this time there was no book on the table.

'Come over here,' he said pulling me towards the other side of the room, where he propped himself on the edge of the bed.

'Sit down,' he said, patting it.

I froze in terror. I'd worked out from TV and from what the white girls in the playground said that when you got into bed with a man he put his willy inside you and that was where babies came from. I'd started watching any TV programmes that showed couples together in the hope of learning more about sex. Dad would switch off if he came into the room, but I'd seen people having pretend sex and I knew it always happened on beds, where the man climbed on top of the woman. Now the imam was going to do it to me. But I didn't want a baby. I was only eleven years old. All I knew was that I mustn't sit down on the bed with him. If I didn't get on the bed, he wouldn't be able to climb on me. My heart was beating so hard I was sure I was going to faint.

'Come sit,' he demanded.

'No.' I shook my head quietly.

The imam was annoyed. He jumped to his feet and pulled me roughly towards him. Grabbing me round the waist, he threw me on top of the bed, then he stood over me with a sick grin on his face.

'There, that's better,' he said, kneeling on either side of me so I was trapped.

He began tugging at the waistband of my trousers and I had never been so frightened in my life, not in all the years he had been bringing me up there. I had to stop him putting his willy inside me, no matter what it took. Suddenly I found my strength and started beating my fists against his chest as hard as I could. It didn't stop him. Still he continued to pull at the elastic waistband of my trousers and yank them down my legs. I grabbed them, trying to pull them back up again, but it was hopeless.

That's when I started crying. Tears streamed down my face, dripping onto the sheet below. I tried to gasp for breath but the air caught at the back of my throat. I wriggled and writhed, trying to get away, but I was trapped.

'Please don't,' I begged through my sobs. 'Leave me alone, please don't hurt me.'

The imam didn't listen. My trousers were around my knees and now he was pulling at my pants.

'No!' I screamed, hitting him hard against the side of his face. My fist momentarily knocked him off-balance but a split second later he was hovering over me again, just inches from my face.

'Be a good girl and do as I tell you,' he whispered hoarsely.

'No!' I wept. 'Please don't!'

He ripped at my knickers until they were down around my knees. For the first time I was naked and exposed for him to see. I cried out but he put his hand over my mouth to silence me, cutting off my breath. I was so frightened that I thought I'd die on the spot.

Now he lay on top of me, his dead weight pinning me to the bed, crushing my ribs. I tried to reach for my trousers but my fingers couldn't get to them. He was panting his foul breath in my ear as he tried to pull his willy out of his pants. I could feel it all hot and hard and I wriggled and struggled just as frantically as I could. I mustn't let him do this horrible thing to me. I had to stop him somehow.

He couldn't get his pants down without using his hand so he took it off my mouth for a moment, and as soon as he did I screamed out loud at the top of my voice.

'Stop that!' he yelled and clapped his hand to my mouth again. My throat closed in sheer panic. I tried to turn my head to the side, to wriggle my hips out of the way, to push him with all my might, but nothing I did was having any effect. This was it, I told myself. I would probably die right now, here in this horrible, stinking little room. I wanted to die. Death would be better than this.

Suddenly I heard a clattering noise downstairs. The imam's eyes widened with fear. He leapt off me. I was stunned because I'd never seen him look frightened before. It took me a few seconds to realise that I was safe. Someone was here.

The imam quickly pulled up his underpants and re-arranged his sarong.

'Get off the bed,' he hissed.

I jumped to my feet and was still pulling up my trousers when I saw a large dark shadow appear in the doorway. Someone had seen us. I noticed a pair of feet, men's feet, still wearing shoes – shiny black shoes. What kind of a man would wear shoes in a mosque?

'Go downstairs!' the imam barked at me.

I looked up at the man and realised it was another imam, an important man who was in charge of all the mosques in the area. I'd seen him a few times before. Unlike our own grubby imam, this other one was clean and well groomed, with fresh white cotton trousers and a smart grey jacket. He wore a triangular white hat on his head and had a long white pointy beard.

The two imams looked at one another without expression and there was an awkward silence. I saw my chance and fled the room, pushing straight past the man in the doorway.

My heart was still pounding as I flew down the stairs into the hall below. He'd seen me beside the bed with my trousers around my knees. The imam's dirty little secret was out. He'd been caught in the act with me and it would surely be the end of his career here. He'd be sent back to Bangladesh in shame. My mind raced through the possibilities.

But what about me? The imam would tell my parents and I'd be disgraced too. My family would disown me. I'd never have a husband or children because everyone would know I was tainted, used goods.

I pushed open the door of the mosque and ran all the way home, so scared I could hardly breathe. There was a pumping sound in my ears and my legs were like jelly. What would happen next? Would he phone my parents straight away? They might even get a call this evening to tell them what I'd been up to. The imam was definitely finished but I'd have to wait to find out my own fate.

Every time the phone rang at home that evening I thought it was the imam with the shoes calling to tell my parents. I was petrified, but part of me felt relief that finally my torment would be over. But there was no phone call from the imam with the shoes.

I went to school the next day, in trepidation that maybe he would have reported it to the head teacher and that I would be called up to explain myself, but no such call came. That evening I sat in the graveyard instead of going to the mosque, thinking surely my parents would know the truth by the time I got home – but they were eating dinner as usual.

The weekend passed without incident and on the Monday I decided I had to go back to the mosque to find out what was going to happen. I waited until the mosque bus was there and the hall was full of children,

and when I went in the imam shook my hand and
greeted me as usual but didn't say anything else.
Throughout the lesson he didn't look at me, and as
soon as lessons finished I sprinted out the door.

Maybe the imam with the shoes had to make a
formal report to somebody before he took action. I
waited days and then weeks for something to happen,
but nothing ever did. At last, I had to accept that it was
going to be brushed under the carpet, and I was devastated. The other imam knew the truth but he'd failed to
protect me. In essence, he'd betrayed me, just like the
dirty imam. The knowledge that someone else knew but
refused to do anything about it made me feel useless,
like a piece of rubbish to be used and thrown away.
After that, I think a part of me died inside.

I felt alone and utterly abandoned when I realised
that no one was going to help me. There was no hope.
I would have to keep suffering until I was able to leave
the mosque. I felt dirty both inside and out and continued to wash myself vigorously every single night. By
now I couldn't break the habit.

I knew that I couldn't go on like this. Whenever I
thought of the imam's grinning face, his pot belly and
his filthy hands, I hated him with all the hatred in my
soul. I couldn't let him touch me again, couldn't go
back up to his office, because next time he truly would
put his willy inside me and that would be that.

One freezing cold night shortly after the attempted
rape I decided I was going to stand up to the imam once
and for all. I sat through the entire lesson rehearsing
what I'd say to him. I pictured myself telling him enough

was enough – he couldn't touch me or hurt me any more. I rehearsed the words over and over.

After the lesson, I lingered when the other children left. A smile spread across the imam's face and he beckoned me upstairs.

'No,' I said. 'I won't.'

'Come here!' he ordered sharply.

I shook my head.

He got to his feet and grabbed at me, pulling me towards him. I squirmed as he tried to touch me.

'No!' I screamed.

The imam stopped what he was doing and looked at me with narrowed eyes. Suddenly, I felt very powerful.

'If you touch me again I'm going to tell my dad on you,' I declared.

The imam threw back his head and laughed loudly. 'But no one's going to believe you! You're only a little girl.'

'Yes, they will! I'll tell my dad exactly what you've been doing to me.'

The imam stopped smiling and a grimace clouded his face. In a whiny voice he mimicked my threat. 'You're going to tell your dad, are you?' he sang.

I wanted to kick him hard in the shin.

'I will!' I said, nodding, but now my bravery was beginning to wane and my hands were shaking.

'Very well then,' he said. 'Let's phone him.'

He grabbed hold of my hand and dragged me upstairs to his office. He walked over to the telephone, picked up the receiver and dialled a number, then waited for someone to answer on the other end. By now I was panicking. This wasn't part of the confrontation I had planned. I'd been pretty sure he would back down when I made my threat.

'Hello, Mohammed?' he asked, shooting me a glance. 'It's the imam here. I've got Nabila with me.'

Oh no, he really was ringing my dad! My mouth felt bone dry. What on earth was he doing? Was he going to confess? My dad would kill us both.

'How are you?' he continued. He was talking to my father as if he didn't have a care in the world. 'And Shazia, is she well?'

How could he be so brazen? I strained to hear what Dad was saying on the other end, but it was impossible to make out.

'How about a donation for the mosque?' he asked cheekily. 'You haven't sent any money lately.' He saw the horror on my face and winked at me. I wanted to kill him.

'Nabila?' he asked, looking at me. I jumped at the mention of my name. 'Oh yes, she's here with me now at the mosque. She's fine.'

I watched him nodding his head as he spoke.

'Yes, yes, that's right, she is.'

What on earth were they talking about?

I felt a warm sensation at the front of my trousers. *No, not again*. I'd wet myself right here in front of him and he'd watched me do it. The imam began to laugh but disguised it, pretending he was laughing at something Dad had said.

I was heartbroken. In that moment I realised that I would never be able to tell anyone what was happening to me. The imam was joking and laughing with my dad as if they were old friends. I imagined my polite and gracious father on the other end of the line. He'd be delighted that the imam, the leader of the community, had phoned him. He would be eager to please this horrible man who was molesting his daughter night after night, behind his back.

The imam nodded. 'I'd love to come to dinner. That's very kind of you. Yes, we must arrange it very soon.'

I allowed the rest of the wee to run down my leg, onto my school socks and over the floor.

'Yes, okay. Goodbye,' he said, replacing the receiver.

The imam looked at me. 'There! Tell your father. Let's see who he believes.'

He looked in disgust at the wet patch on my trousers and the puddle on the floor. 'You can clean that up before you leave.'

I'd just hit rock bottom. I was less than worthless. I'd tried to stand up to the imam and be strong and tough with him, and instead I had wet myself right in front of him. I was a big baby with wet knickers, worse than useless. Everyone would know how dirty and smelly I was. Everyone would call me a baby and no one would want to be my friend, not even Farqad. They'd all hate me and no one would help me. The imam with the shoes hadn't helped me and he was the most important man I knew.

The imam was right. No one would ever believe me now. He'd won.

Chapter 19

The Special Dinner

A week later, on a balmy summer's evening, I was lying on my bed looking up at my Kylie posters when I heard the front doorbell chime. I glanced at my watch and saw it was after eight o'clock. Who could be visiting us so late at night?

I heard Mum scurrying from the kitchen and along the hallway to answer the door, then there were men's voices below. I crept out of my bedroom and sneaked along to the top of the stairs so I could hear more. One voice sounded familiar. Suddenly, terror gripped me and I became rooted to the spot. It was the imam, chatting to my dad.

The voices faded as the men moved along the hallway and into the front room.

I'd noticed that Dad hadn't eaten much at dinner earlier and then that Mum was chopping up all the ingredients for her special chicken curry, but I hadn't thought to ask who she was making it for. Now it all made sense – she'd been cooking for the imam.

My head began to pound with anger. How dare he come here? It was my home, my sanctuary. I only felt safe from him here and at school, but now he was downstairs, just feet below me. He was in my house, with my family, invading and tarnishing my life here just as he had done at the mosque. I felt like retching when I thought of his stinking breath and body polluting the lovely clean air downstairs; of my parents fussing around him, bowing and scraping to the man who had ruined my life. It was as though the noose was tightening around me. It seemed there was nowhere I could go to escape this man.

My palms were sweaty on the banister as I inched down the steps. I had to know what they were talking about. Was he going to tell Dad what he did to me at the mosque? My heart was in my mouth.

Eventually, I reached the bottom step and sat still, in such a trance that I didn't even notice Mum appear by my side.

'Oh, you're there!' she exclaimed. 'I've been calling you. Didn't you hear? Come into the kitchen and help me with the food. The imam's here, so it has to be right.'

My stomach flipped at the smell of the cooking. Mum had prepared two plates of curry and she'd even got out the best china to impress the imam. If only they knew what he was really like; if only they knew him as well as I did.

'Take these through,' she ordered. 'Quick, hurry up, we don't want to keep the imam waiting.'

But I was afraid. I didn't want to see him. I didn't want to come face to face with the man who touched and hurt me night after night. The thought that he was only in the next room made me shiver with fear.

'Don't let his food get cold,' she said, wiping her hands on her apron as I hesitated. 'It'll be nice for him to see you.' She gave me a shove towards the door.

I shuddered. I wanted to creep back upstairs, curl up on my bed and pretend the imam wasn't here. I knew that once I saw him, sitting at our family table, the image would always be there in my head. I'd never feel safe in my own home again.

'Can't *you* take the food in to them?' I begged Mum.

'No, I can't. What's wrong with you?'

Mum ran her hand through her hair and wiped the back of it against her forehead. The hot stove had made her sweat and there were beads of perspiration on her forehead. 'I can't let him see me like this, can I? No, you take the food in. Hurry up!'

She was beginning to get annoyed so I did as I was told. I leant my elbow against the handle of the dining-room door, pushing it down so the door swung open. Immediately I felt his eyes on me. I felt awkward and wondered if he felt the same, but I didn't say a word. I refused to look at him. Instead I put the plates down on the table. I wanted to spit in his food, right in the middle of his curry. He was an animal.

I could feel his eyes burning into my back as I left the room.

'Thank you, Nabila,' Dad called.

Through the door I heard the men beginning to eat. I sat on the bottom step, trying to eavesdrop, but the voices were too muffled and distorted. Suddenly I heard the sound of laughter. They wouldn't be laughing if he had told Dad about all the dirty things we had been up to. Maybe my secret was safe for now.

Wearily, I climbed upstairs to my bed and hid beneath the covers. My body trembled in the darkness as I lay there waiting for the imam to leave. I listened for the sound of the front door closing behind him, of his footsteps on the street outside. I should have changed and got into bed but I was scared. I had to stay fully clothed. There was no way I was taking my pants off with the imam sitting feet below me in the room downstairs.

It was almost ten-thirty when he finally left. I heard his voice in the hallway as Dad opened the front door and bade him goodnight.

'Don't forget to send Nabila with that donation now, will you?' I heard him urge as he turned into the street outside.

'I won't,' Dad called.

I pulled back the edge of my bedroom curtain, being careful not to move it too much because I didn't want the imam to see my frightened face at the window. The shadowy figure walked off into the night and I remained there watching until I couldn't see him any more. Only then did I feel safe enough to change into my pyjamas and go to bed.

That evil man had taken over every area of my life. He'd made me do horrible and disgusting things to him and had stolen my innocence; he'd ruined my friendships by beating and trying to abuse my friends; and now he'd invaded my home – my sanctuary. I didn't feel safe here any more – not even in my own bedroom. The imam was everywhere. There was no escape from him and there never would be as long as I stayed at the mosque.

Something inside me gave up that night. I padded quietly to the bathroom, locked the door and began to scrub at my skin. I felt dirty just because he'd been near. His stinking breath had breathed the same air as me and now it was on my skin. I needed to wash it off. I had to scour him away. Only then could I rest – only then could I feel clean again.

The following morning, my eyes followed Dad like a hawk. Did he know anything? Did he look at me any differently? But he seemed exactly the same as usual.

I watched and waited, but nothing. Dad was his usual cheery self whilst Mum was humming to herself in the kitchen. The imam hadn't said a word, but his visit had terrified me and he'd known it would. This was just another way of punishing me, of showing me how much power he had, that he could come freely into my home and treat my dad like an old friend.

If he could do that, he could do anything. Something had to be done.

Chapter 20

The Card in
the Kitchen

Picking up the prayer book, I flicked through to the end. I was eleven years old, nearly twelve, and I'd almost finished learning the Koran. Soon it would be time to leave the mosque and I was counting the days.

It was getting close to the end of the school year and my last day at the mosque would coincide with the beginning of the six-week summer holidays. Sadly, it also meant saying goodbye to my lovely friend Farqad. I was going to miss her but we lived in different parts of town and went to different schools so I knew I'd be unlikely to see her again.

I was the oldest, so I'd be the first of our crowd of girls to leave. I wondered who his next victim would be. The thought plagued me because I didn't want anyone else to suffer. Now that Wafa had gone, there was no one else who was young, pretty and girly. Maybe I'd be his final victim. I convinced myself that it would all stop when I left.

As it was, he'd not tried to touch me since the night of the attempted rape. Maybe it had frightened him in some way. Maybe, even though the imam in the shoes had said nothing, just him walking in on us like that was enough to make the imam stop for good. Gradually I dared to hope that I was safe.

I wondered whether I should tell someone about the abuse once I was no longer there to face the consequences, but the more I thought about it, the more it scared me because I knew, whoever I told, it would leak out and I would be disgraced. Besides, no one would ever believe me. They would never take the word of a child against that of an imam.

I wished I were stronger, braver and older so that I could stand up to him. If he ever did this to another girl, it would be all my fault. I'd be guilty. I prayed that wouldn't happen.

Finally my last day at the mosque arrived. I walked in to find the imam waiting for me in the hallway.

'Come on,' he said, grabbing at my hand, 'I've got something to show you.'

I closed my eyes and gritted my teeth: this would be the final time he ever touched me. '*Get through this and you will be a survivor,*' I told myself.

The imam took me upstairs, but instead of going straight to his bedroom he led me into the kitchen, where he walked over to the fridge. With a bit of effort he pulled it away from the wall, leaned behind it and retrieved something.

'Here,' he announced, holding out a large square white box. 'This is for you!' Excitement flashed across his eyes as he handed it to me.

I studied it. There was no writing on it, nothing to give me a clue what was inside.

'Well, open it then!' he urged impatiently.

I prised off the lid and peered inside. It was a gold shiny card with one large raised heart, surrounded by lots of tiny red ones. I tried to hide my repulsion. It was exactly the sort of cheap padded card a boy would give to his girlfriend on Valentine's Day. If a boy my own age had given it to me, I would have been delighted. As it was, it was from the imam. And now he stood before me, grinning, waiting for me to open it up and read what was inside.

My stomach lurched as I read the black handwriting inside. Although by now the imam could speak a few words of broken English, he always spoke to us in Urdu. But here, in a childlike scrawl, were English words, which he'd managed to translate. It was as though it was his final gift to me. It read: 'To Nabila, I have enjoyed teaching you. I will be missing you. Lots of love from your teacher.' Underneath, he'd signed off with dozens of kisses.

I felt sick. Lots of love? He'd abused me for almost five years and yet he was sending me a padded card as if we were boyfriend and girlfriend. Did he know I was supposed to be marrying Fajr's brother? Had Dad told him when they had dinner that night? You shouldn't send cards like this to someone who was betrothed to another. Teachers shouldn't send them to their pupils.

'What do you think?' he asked eagerly.

'It's nice,' I smiled weakly. What else could I say?

He stood there waiting for more.

'Thank you,' I whispered. I didn't mean it. I felt sick saying the words.

The imam wrapped his arms around me and I flinched. I shut my eyes and prepared for the worst, but instead of his hands on my body I felt a warm wet kiss on the top of my head. I waited for something worse, but nothing happened. Instead we stood there together, with me locked in his embrace.

'You've been such a brilliant student,' he said wistfully.

I was horrified. He was completely mad if he thought it was normal to send a love card to a child. He was sick in the head. He clearly thought we were in a relationship and that he was my boyfriend. Thank goodness this was my last day; thank goodness I was getting out.

'Just make sure you take it with you when you go,' he added. 'I'll put it back behind the fridge and you can collect it later. It's our secret.'

He wedged the card firmly behind the fridge and put his finger to his lips as if to shush me.

I couldn't stop thinking about the card as I sat downstairs during lessons. Farqad was emotional about me going and I began to worry that maybe the imam might start abusing her after I left. I felt protective towards her and agonised over whether I should tell her about him. I wanted to, very much. The words were there, in my head, waiting to be spoken, but I was frightened of what would happen to me and my family if I did. I was also concerned for Farqad. She'd still have to go to the mosque, and maybe by telling her I'd put her at even greater risk. If the imam thought she knew, he'd make her his next target just to keep her quiet. My shame would become hers. I couldn't do that to her; she was my friend. In the end, I decided not to breathe a word to anyone, not ever.

Suddenly the imam called out my name. 'Nabila, I need you to clean the kitchen.'

I stood up and looked around the room. 'Can someone come and help me, please?'

I expected him to say no and so did everyone else, but he surprised us all. 'Yes, okay,' he agreed. 'Take a few of the others with you.'

I grabbed Farqad's hand and glanced along the row of girls, all of whom wanted to get out of prayers and were pleading with their eyes for me to pick them. I caught eyes with the two girls who'd been mean to me, who'd called me the 'chosen one'.

'Come on,' I said. 'You can help too.' It felt like a day for building bridges.

Soon all four of us were in the kitchen cleaning, scrubbing and giggling. I glanced at my watch: one more hour and I'd be out of this place for good. I couldn't wait. My heart felt light. The nightmare was ending. I was almost free – free to be the little girl I used to be before I met the imam.

'You're so lucky,' one of the girls said.

'I know!' I answered. I could barely wipe the smile from my face.

'Do you know,' she said, 'we always wanted to be your friend but we didn't think you liked us very much.'

I turned to her in astonishment. 'I thought *you* didn't like *me*,' I spluttered.

She shook her head and put down her cloth. 'It wasn't that. It was just that you are so pretty and you were chosen to do everything for the imam – we wanted to be like you, didn't we?' She looked over at her friend and the other girl nodded back in confirmation.

I was flabbergasted. They didn't have a clue what I'd been through. If they had, there's no way they'd want to stand in my shoes. I turned to focus on cleaning the worktop so they didn't see the tears in my eyes.

Just then, the imam walked in. 'Hmm,' he said, looking around the kitchen, 'almost finished in here. Nabila, why don't you clean the toilet before you go?'

I did as he asked, and scrubbed that toilet until it was sparkling, then gave it a flush for the very last time.

Back downstairs again, I saw Farqad and the two girls whispering in a corner. 'You're not going to believe it!' one of them gasped as I sat down. 'It's the imam,' she said. 'He's got a girlfriend!'

My stomach twisted. Did they mean me? What did they know? 'How did you find out? Who is she?' I demanded, a little too quickly.

Farqad took up the story: 'We found a card stuffed behind the fridge in the kitchen.'

This was it, the moment I'd been dreading. I'd been found out, but not just by anyone – I'd been found out by my friends. I could barely look at them. They giggled over their juicy piece of gossip.

'What did it say – the card?' I pressed.

The girls rolled their eyes.

'That's the thing,' Farqad explained. 'I'd just got it out to have a look when the imam walked in so I had to stuff it back behind the fridge quickly!'

I let out a silent sigh of relief. *They hadn't read it, thank goodness.*

'What did it look like?' I asked. 'How can you be sure he's got a girlfriend?'

'It was smothered in little hearts,' one of the girls said. 'That's how we know. It was a big padded thing, like a Valentine's card. We're gonna try and sneak another look at it later, before we go home.'

I felt the blood in my veins turn to ice. I had to get to the card before they did.

The rest of the lesson dragged on for an eternity. I watched the second hand as it ticked slowly round the huge clock. How could I retrieve the card before they did?

I glanced up at the imam, trying to attract his attention. I needed to get out of this lesson now but he didn't look my way, not even once.

Finally, I couldn't wait any longer.

'Can I be excused, please?' I asked, raising my hand.

The imam craned his neck to look at the clock behind him.

'As it's your last day, you might as well go now,' he said.

I nodded gratefully. I don't know what I was expecting: some sort of recognition for everything I'd done for him, I suppose. Instead, he looked straight back down at the prayer book.

'Goodbye, Nabila,' Farqad whispered.

'Goodbye,' I said, touching her on the shoulder as I got up to leave.

I walked out through the mosque door and into the hallway. I was careful to shut the door behind me before squatting down to fasten my shoes. The stairs to the kitchen were slightly to my left, but I couldn't go up immediately in case someone heard me. Instead, I made a huge show of banging the main front door of the mosque loudly behind me as I stepped into the street outside.

As I did so, I took a deep breath of fresh air to calm my pounding heart. I should have been elated – I was free at last! But as long as that card was in the kitchen I was still his prisoner. I felt crippled with anxiety.

I stood on the pavement outside the mosque considering what to do next. I couldn't risk leaving it there because the girls would go and find it at the end of the lesson. I had to return one more time; it was the only solution. Moments later, I opened the door slightly and squeezed through the gap, being careful not to let it bang shut.

I took off my shoes and held them in my hands as I tiptoed up the stairs. All I could hear was the rush of blood in my brain. My body felt as if it was running on adrenaline. I had to be quiet and I had to be fast.

I reached the top of the stairs, went into the kitchen and tiptoed over to the fridge. The metal behind it was hot and burnt my arm, and it was difficult to extract the box because of the way it was wedged in, but finally I managed to get a grip and pull it out. The cardboard was scraped and damaged, but I didn't care. I hated this card and everything it stood for. Now I needed to throw it away if I was ever to be free of the imam.

I crept quietly back down the stairs again and sneaked out through the mosque door. Stopping only to slip my feet into my shoes, I raced off down the main road and into the graveyard. The dead had been my friends when things were at their worst. This place had been my sanctuary on the long, dark nights when the abuse had become too much to bear. I kept on running until the gate was in sight, my shoes slopping around because I hadn't even stopped to fasten them.

Just by the exit, I spotted a bin. I crushed the card in two and pushed it deep down into the rubbish. It would remain hidden there amongst the rotting flowers, food wrappers and cigarette ends until the council came and emptied it into a huge landfill site, where it would be covered with tons of earth, never to be seen again. It would be buried for good – the imam's dirty secret gone forever.

I was elated as I walked the rest of the way home. I wanted to dance and sing in the street, to call out and share the joy in my heart. After almost five years of abuse, I'd been released from my prison. The chains that shackled me had gone and I'd never have to see the imam again. The sun was shining in the sky. It felt like a new beginning. It was finally over. I was free.

Chapter 21

Being
Found Out

I looked forward to my future without the imam, and the start of the six-week school holidays. When I went back I'd be starting secondary school but meanwhile I had the whole long summer in front of me and everything was perfect.

A couple of weeks after I'd left the mosque, Mum and I got a call inviting us over to Wafa's house. Her mother had telephoned specially to ask us and I was looking forward to it. I'd not seen Wafa for a couple of months, not since she'd left the mosque. I was looking forward to chatting and playing with her now that I was a normal girl again, without all the pressure I'd been under.

Wafa's mum opened the door and as I peered past her looking for my friend I noticed there wasn't the usual smile or cheery hello and felt a strange tension in the air. Something was wrong. Wafa's mum was usually very friendly towards me but today she was cold and blunt.

'She's through there,' she said, her voice sounding abrupt, off-hand almost.

Seconds later, Wafa came running from the kitchen into the hallway. Unlike her mum, my friend was her usual bubbly self.

'Hello, Nabila, come upstairs and we can play with my tea-set. I'll even let you pour the tea.'

But I couldn't take my eyes off Wafa's mother. A cold chill ran through me. There was an atmosphere in the air. Something had changed. A small knot of anxiety twisted like a blunt knife in the pit of my stomach. I didn't want to go and play. I wanted to stay downstairs and hear what the adults had to say, but Wafa was pulling at my arm impatiently.

'Come on, slow coach!' she teased.

'Go on,' Mum said, shooing me away.

Wafa's mum usually offered me something to eat or drink, but this time she simply walked into the kitchen and began stirring a pot of curry that was on the stove. My mum followed and sat down at the table, then they pushed the door closed, making it clear that children would not be privy to this conversation.

This seemed ominous and I was scared as I dragged my feet up the stairs to Wafa's bedroom.

'Here, I've set up the table. You get the dolls from over there and we can start the party,' she said happily.

But my mind was downstairs with the two mums. Wafa repeated herself, beginning to get cross with me.

I grabbed the dolls and shoved them against the table, but my heart wasn't in it. I didn't want to play; I wanted to be down there, in the adult world. Somehow I knew that they would be talking about the imam. It was the only possible reason for her mum's coldness. Wafa must have told her what happened when I caught him touching her in his office. What did she know about me? Had Wafa told her mum that I offered myself to him in her place?

I felt sick. My palms were hot and sweaty as we went through the motions of pouring pretend tea and eating slices of imaginary cake. We played for a while until Wafa tired of it.

'All done. Let's go and play outside!' she cried, jumping to her feet.

I ran downstairs with her, but as we went through the kitchen I purposely stopped to look at Mum. As soon as we entered the room, the two women stopped talking. Something was definitely going on.

'Come on, Nabila, let's go!' Wafa insisted, pulling at my clothes.

She continued out through the back door into the garden, but I was petrified. I waited for someone to say something but they just sat there in complete silence. I needed a sign that everything was all right but no one said a word. Mum's eyes remained firmly glued to the ground.

'Nabila, go outside,' she snapped, her voice terse and edgy. Was she cross with me about something Wafa's mum had told her?

I looked out the back door at Wafa on the swing, sailing through the air as if she didn't have a care in the world. Should I ask her if she had said something? I didn't know what to do or say.

Suddenly, Mum's voice broke the silence. 'Nabila, are you deaf?' she shouted. 'I said GO OUTSIDE!'

As I walked to the back door my legs turned to jelly. I thought my nightmare at the mosque had ended the day I left, but now it was beginning all over again. My mind raced. If they knew, how much did they know? I'd thought I was free of him but he was still there inside my head, tormenting me daily. I'd just started to feel like a normal little girl again but now I realised things could never be normal for me again. The imam had left a stain on me that weighed heavy on my heart, one I would never be able to shift.

I went outside and played with Wafa for another hour before Mum called to me that it was time to go home. I went upstairs to help Wafa put her toys away, then as Mum and I headed for the front door I turned to smile at Wafa's mum, but she refused to look at me. It was as though I was invisible. I tried to read her face and she seemed embarrassed, unsure of what to say. She definitely knew. I was certain of it.

'See you soon,' Wafa chirped, as she waved at me from the doorstep.

'Bye,' I whispered as the door closed behind us.

My mother marched off up the street at breakneck speed like a woman on a mission. Was she angry with me? I couldn't tell. I ran to try and catch up with her but when I did she quickened her pace and walked even faster. I tried to make eye contact but her eyes were fixed straight ahead. I wanted to ask what was wrong, but at the same time I didn't want to know. I began to chatter about other things but she wasn't listening. Even though it was a scorching hot day, I shivered. How much did she know? What would I say to her? Would she tell Dad?

The more I searched her face for an answer, the faster she walked. We were almost at the house when Mum suddenly whirled around to face me. She grabbed my arm roughly, her eyes wild with anger.

'Why didn't you tell me?' she hissed, a look of utter disgust on her face.

She didn't elaborate; she didn't have to. It was obvious she knew all about the imam and me. I felt sick and filthy all at the same time.

I realised in a flash that Wafa had told her mother everything. It had been a couple of months since I'd last seen her, and I guessed she must have been making excuses to her mother all that time so she wouldn't be sent back to the mosque. Her mum probably nagged and nagged her to go and finally she broke down and described what happened that time when the imam touched her, and my part in all of it. She was a brave little girl. If only I'd been as brave.

My heart pounded. What did Mum think? Could she possibly imagine that I was a willing victim of the imam and that I'd somehow enjoyed it? Why did she seem so cross with me?

'I … I …' I stammered, trying to find an answer.

Mum snorted and turned sharply on her heel. I watched as she marched up to our front door and disappeared inside, leaving it open for me. It swung sadly as if inviting me to the next chapter of my life.

My secret was out. I'd always longed to tell my parents but I'd never dreamt they would find out like this. For all those years I'd desperately hoped that someone would come along and rescue me, but they hadn't. Now Mum knew everything and she blamed me, just as I had always feared she would. If only Wafa could have kept my secret then everything would have been okay.

Would Mum tell Dad? What would he think of his beautiful little girl doing horrible, disgusting things with the imam? I'd brought shame on the family. I'd be cast out. No one would want me any more.

Distraught, I ran into the house and bolted straight upstairs to my bedroom, where I buried my face in the pillow and began to cry bitterly. Downstairs I could hear my parents' raised voices. Dad was shouting and Mum was wailing. Of course she would tell him. She told him everything. I tried to imagine what she was saying about me. I'd seen that look of disgust on her face. I only hoped that my brothers were out so that they wouldn't hear this too. I wanted to die of shame.

A couple of hours later Mum called me for dinner and I trudged warily downstairs. My brothers were round the table and I didn't know who knew and who didn't, which made things even worse. As soon as I walked into the dining room I wanted the ground to swallow me up. I felt all eyes on me, even though when I finally looked up Dad was staring straight ahead. My face was flushed as I took my place. Mum walked briskly into the room and slammed the plates in front of us. She looked red-eyed, as if she'd been crying.

The food was piping hot and smelt delicious but I couldn't eat a thing. I felt sick to the stomach that my secret was out.

Mum took her place at the dinner table and we began to eat in silence. I sneaked a look at Dad and his face was tired and old, with sadness in his eyes – sadness and disappointment. I was the one who had caused that disappointment.

I wondered whether they would talk to the imam about this. Surely I wasn't the only one to blame? I was a child while he was the adult.

The meal was excruciating. I hardly touched a scrap of food on my plate. Instead I pushed it around with my fork until it was all messed up.

Suddenly Dad's voice broke the silence. 'Nabila, go to your room.'

I couldn't wait to get out of there. Keeping my head bowed I left the room, but I hung around in the hall outside to listen to what was being said.

'From now on, I don't want you to wrestle with your sister any more,' I heard Dad saying to my brothers. 'She's too old for it.'

We'd always enjoyed tussling, rolling around the ground, and Dad often joined in, so surely they would think it odd that he had banned it so suddenly? I waited for them to ask why, but no one said a word. Did that mean they knew?

The silence made me feel worse. From now on I'd be treated differently by my own family, and I hated it. They were ashamed of me even though they probably only knew a small fraction of the story. I imagined that

Wafa had told her mum about the imam touching her, but still no one knew what he had done to me. No one knew that he used to pleasure himself and spill his horrible white stuff all over my hand, that he used to shove his dirty finger inside me and play with my private parts till they were red and painful, and that he tried to put his willy inside me. Still no one knew about that, thank goodness. I'd been right not to tell anyone. Mum would be even more furious with me if she knew about that disgusting stuff.

Although Dad was head of the household, it was Mum who was in charge. Dad was a typical Muslim husband – he went out to work so that he could provide for his family, but it was Mum's job to keep us children under control. Dad only ever got involved when we'd done something really bad. But this was something really bad and now he knew.

I despised the imam for what he'd done to me and my family. I wished he could be punished for it, but I would never tell anyone else if this was the kind of reaction I could expect. Without the support of my parents I would never be able to bring him to justice on my own. Far from taking my side, my parents felt I had brought shame on them and stained the family name. They wanted it swept under the carpet and kept quiet.

I'd disgraced myself. This was my fault. It was all my doing and now I was going to be punished. I would be forever alone with my secret.

Chapter 22

An Arranged Future

After they learned my secret, my parents looked at me in a different way. I wasn't their little girl any more and they treated me with a coldness that was palpable. I had wondered whether they might go to the imam and confront him, at least tell him what they thought of him, but they didn't. Instead they did nothing at all. They couldn't live with the shame. From now on, this would be a family secret. It had gone from being my secret to one the whole family shared. It was so unfair. I hadn't asked to be chosen by the imam. It wasn't my fault, yet I was being treated as if it was.

I wanted Dad to storm into the mosque and punch the imam in the face. But he didn't. His little girl was soiled goods. Now they'd have to keep the imam's dirty secret for him because otherwise everyone would find out about me and then they'd never be able to marry me off. Fajr's brother would run a mile. I would remain

unmarriageable, like a lead weight hanging around
their necks for the rest of their lives.

Mum seemed to want me out of the house, out of her
sight. I wondered if it was because I disgusted her, or
because having me around was a constant reminder of
what had happened. I didn't know why she was acting
the way she was but it made me feel much worse.
Sometimes I felt like trying to explain to her that I had
been a victim, and asking her what I could have done
differently, but I was too embarrassed to bring it up. I
felt angry with her as well because it was as if she was
punishing me, as if I hadn't been punished enough by
what I'd been through.

There was nothing I could do to make amends. Well,
maybe only one thing: I upped the self-harm to the next
level. I'd stopped washing myself obsessively the day I
left the mosque but now I began slashing myself with
razors again. The torment never stopped. I shredded my
legs to ribbons, being careful to cut where no one would
see the scars.

One day, Mum and Dad told me they had decided I
should go to Newcastle for part of the school holidays
to stay with Habib's in-laws. I think the family wanted
to see what I was like, to check whether I would make
a good wife for their son one day. Before he'd found out
about the abuse, my father had always refused their
request, saying that he would worry about me too
much being up there on my own, but now that I was
damaged goods it was as if he had given up worrying
about me. After all, I'd come to harm right underneath
their noses.

All I could think about was what a relief it would be to spend two weeks away from my parents' disapproving stares over the dinner table. I wasn't sure if my brothers knew about what the imam had done to me but I prayed they didn't. The thought of them knowing was too much to bear.

I'd heard that our in-laws were a modern, forward-thinking Asian family and was excited at the thought of staying with them. I threw all my best clothes into a suitcase. This would be a holiday for me, time away from my parents and my shame. I'd be with people who didn't know about the imam, people who didn't know my dirty secret. This was my chance for a fresh start.

Fajr had two sisters who were married and lived in the same house with their husbands and children. There were four children altogether, aged between two and eight years old. Although much younger than me the little girls were allowed to cut their hair and wear it with a fashionable fringe at the front. Instead of being given chores to do in the kitchen, I was free to go out and play with them in the street. I spent two wonderful weeks laughing, playing and being pampered by the family. The women loved to dress me up and, since I was the oldest of the children, they put me in charge. It was a lovely family and I felt excited at the thought that I might become part of it one day if I married the younger brother. I still hadn't met him but if he was as nice as his sisters, then surely things would be fine.

When they saw how happy I was, the family rang my father to ask if they could keep me for an extra week. I crossed my fingers as I eavesdropped on the phone call. I expected him to say 'no' but to my amazement he agreed.

Sadly, at the end of the third week I was summoned home. I was gutted because I wanted to stay in Newcastle forever, away from the weight of my guilt. Back home, Dad nagged me to read the Koran, but prayers were the last thing on my mind. I didn't have to go to the mosque any more, but every time I recited my prayers I could feel the imam's hot breath on my neck. The holy words brought it all flooding back into a sharp and painful focus.

Whilst Dad nagged me to go to my bedroom and recite my prayers, Mum would try and shoo me out of the front door.

'Go and play, Nabila. Get out of my hair for a few hours,' she'd moan.

Before they found out about the imam, Mum hadn't liked me hanging around the streets with the other kids, but now she was throwing me out at every available opportunity.

'Why don't you go and call for Suki?' she suggested one Friday morning. 'You haven't seen her for ages.'

I watched in the mirror as she applied some black mascara. Why was she getting dolled up and where was she going without me?

There were only the two of us in the house. Dad had left earlier that morning to go to prayers at the mosque he attended, which was in a different part of town. He'd been going there for years because that's where his friends went.

My brothers were also out and Mum made it perfectly clear that she wanted to be alone. But why was she wearing full make-up if she was just staying in?

The answer came not long afterwards. I left the house and headed towards Suki's house. As I walked along I spotted Aariz, our old neighbour from the shop, lurking at the bottom of our street. He was on the other side of the road but I looked over and smiled politely. Strangely, he didn't smile back. Instead he ignored me and pulled a newspaper up around his face. I thought it odd because he always wanted to stop and have a chat.

A shudder ran through me. Did he know about my disgrace? Was he blanking me because I was shameful? If so, I knew it wouldn't be long before he'd tell everyone. I shuddered at the thought.

I ran the rest of the way to Suki's house, where I spent the remainder of the day, but I couldn't shake the uneasy feeling I'd got seeing Aariz like that. The following Friday, just after Dad left for the mosque, the same thing happened again. I saw Aariz walking very slowly up the road towards our house. I wanted to shout over to him but his eyes remained fixed firmly ahead. He was taking such small steps that he looked ridiculous. Why was he acting so strangely? I decided to wait at the end of the road and hide so that I could watch him. Once I was out of sight, I saw Aariz check both ways before running across the road and up to our front door. It would've been funny if it hadn't been so bizarre.

Mum opened the door, checked up and down the street that the coast was clear, then let him in. What the hell was going on? Mum's face was plastered in make-up and now she was letting an old neighbour into the house when *Dad* wasn't even there. Something was wrong. Determined to find out, I stormed back home and tried the handle but the door was locked from the inside. Mum had put the chain across, something she never did.

I banged loudly on the door but there was no reply. I knocked some more and pressed the doorbell repeatedly until she finally appeared. As she opened the door I noticed that her clothes were slightly dishevelled. She was furious when she saw me standing on the doorstep.

'What on earth do you want?' she snapped. 'I thought you'd gone to call for Suki.'

'She wasn't in,' I lied, pushing past her. I knew Aariz was there and I was determined to find him.

I went straight to the kitchen, but there was no sign. Mum followed me in a panic. The back door was wide open and swinging in the breeze. He'd escaped just in time. I turned to face Mum, who lowered her eyes and blushed slightly. I'd caught her red-handed.

'What about some of your other friends?' she spluttered, trying to keep calm.

'There's no one about,' I said, eyeing her, 'so I thought I'd just come home. Why – is that a problem?'

'No, no. It's not a problem, of course not!' She smiled, tidying back loose strands of hair from her face.

I felt furious with her. Was she really having an affair with Aariz? She must be. How could she do that to Dad?

Nothing more was said but it was obvious what was going on, and now she knew that I knew the atmosphere between us was even more strained. It looked as though Mum and Aariz had been carrying on their affair every Friday while Dad was at the mosque saying his prayers. I couldn't believe it. She'd judged me when she found out about the imam, and had laid the blame entirely at my feet. Now here she was seeing someone else in broad daylight. She was such a hypocrite. That day I lost a lot of respect for my mother.

I pondered whether I should I tell Dad about it. He had a right to know. I thought about it a lot but I couldn't decide the words I would use to tell him, and when I imagined the hurt look on his face I knew I couldn't do it. He was fifty-two years old and starting to look his age, while Mum was aged thirty-seven and still young and attractive. What good would come of him knowing about the affair? They would never get divorced. They would still live together but in misery. Besides, who was I to take the moral high ground? I was the black sheep of the family, not the shining example of good behaviour. I had to leave well alone, but it caused a new rift in my already difficult relationship with Mum.

September finally arrived and I started at my new school. I loved secondary school from the very first day because it gave me a sense of freedom that I'd never experienced before. The teachers treated us as grown-ups. Unlike at home, I could make my own choices.

When I started, my three oldest brothers had already left. Habib was married, of course, and living in Pakistan. Tariq had joined the army at the age of sixteen and had already been gone a year. Saeed had left home before him but continued to drift in and out of our lives. He became a mechanic and got himself a white girlfriend, much to my parents' horror, but whenever he ran out of money he'd be back, knocking on the door for help. Asif was still at school but Mum and Dad had pretty much given up on him as he was always sneaking off out with his mates. It annoyed me because I wasn't ever allowed out at night. Asif was behaving badly while I had been a victim, but it was me, not him, who was being punished by our parents. I was seen as the one who'd brought shame upon our family.

A year after their marriage, Habib and his wife Fajr came to live with us at the family home, and right from the start I adored her. She was beautiful and young and she soon became like the sister I'd never had. I hung on her every word. She was keen that I should marry her younger brother and often talked to me about the life I would lead. My dad was fond of Fajr's family, and as I grew to love Fajr I imagined I would grow to love her brother as well.

'You'll never have to work, Nabila,' she promised me. 'You'll have everything. There will be so much money!'

She made it all sound very glamorous but I knew I'd have a strict life, living amongst her family and bringing up children of my own. Besides, I still felt very apprehensive about having a husband. I knew I would never be able to have sex without being overwhelmed by memories of my experiences with the imam. Besides, I worried that a future husband would be able to tell I'd been abused. I wasn't sure what physical damage had been done to me by his prodding and probing, never mind the mental scars. All my friends had started their periods except for me and I fretted that the imam had damaged me inside. Fortunately, my periods started during that first year of secondary school, and that was a relief. My friends all used tampons but I wouldn't because the thought of putting something inside me brought flashbacks to the abuse.

Anyway, there was to be no getting out of the marriage with Fajr's brother. Dad had given his word, so it was as good as set in stone.

'You will marry when you leave school at sixteen,' he told me. 'I want you to complete your studies first and then you can become a married woman.'

I couldn't argue. I felt I'd already brought so much shame upon my family that I'd have to do as they wanted and try to make them proud of me again.

Chapter 23

Rebellion

I kept my old friends at secondary school but made lots of new ones as well. Boys began to pay attention to me, and I liked it. I suppose it made me feel loved and wanted. I'd flirt back but I never let it go any further. The thought of being close to a boy filled me with horror. If they asked me out I always turned them down. In the end, they saw me as more of a mate than girlfriend material.

I'd sit next to boys during lessons, but they didn't make me nervous. I somehow knew that they wouldn't hurt me the way the imam had. I could tell that they were different from him, that they were kind and could be trusted. They were just innocent boys, not far out of childhood, and would never have dreamed of trying to do the sordid things he'd done to me. I'd been abused but I'd survived. *If I could get through that*, I told myself, *I could get through anything.*

I was still self-harming at home but far less than I used to, because the stability and contentment I felt at school touched every part of my life. It wasn't long before I stopped cutting myself with razors altogether – although every time I felt stressed I remembered the sense of relief it used to give me. I was terrified that it would rear its ugly head once more and I would start all over again. The urge to harm was always there, waiting in the back of my mind, threatening to overwhelm me, but somehow my happiness had made me stronger so I fought the urge and kept it at bay. Occasionally I'd catch myself pinching or scratching my face because it had become a habit, but I'd stop as soon as I realised what I was doing.

Mum and Dad made me wear trousers to school. I longed to wear a skirt and was envious of all the other girls around me. My school trousers were hot and itchy but at least they hid the old scars on my legs. The only exception to the rule was games. I wasn't supposed to, but one day I wore a short green gym skirt that the PE teacher had lent me. Mum would've gone mad if she'd seen me, but she wasn't there and I didn't care. I couldn't miss my only chance of wearing one. Instead, I pulled my long socks up over my scarred legs and hitched the skirt right up, high around my waist. I loved being just like the other girls.

Gradually, my desire to be just like my school friends began to overwhelm me. One Saturday, a year after starting secondary school, I closed my bedroom door and took out a pair of Mum's scissors. Laying some newspaper on the ground, I began to snip away at my hair to create a fringe, like the ones all the other girls had. Soon long strands of black hair lay on the floor at my feet. I regarded myself in the mirror and was pleased with the effect, but then I heard Mum moving around downstairs. She'd go mad when she saw what I'd done.

I folded the newspaper in on itself with the hair inside and shoved it to the bottom of my bin. Taking a comb, I pulled my new fringe to either side and tucked it neatly behind each ear. I combed the side bits forward, so it looked as though I'd just tied it back. I had masses of hair, so it was easy to disguise the cut. Later that day I went down to the kitchen to test it out, but Mum was too busy clattering pots and pans to look at me properly. I'd got away with it!

It was a week before she noticed. She came into the kitchen while I was making toast and said, 'I know what you've done,' while pulling at my hair.

My heart missed a beat. I waited for her to start ranting and raving but instead she just shook her head and tutted. I was growing up, making my own decisions, and there was nothing she could do about it.

Things were becoming strained at home. Habib and Fajr were always bickering with my parents. They still tried to rule Habib's life but Fajr was having none of it, and one day she decided she'd had enough and they moved out to a place of their own so they could start a family. I was upset to see them go.

'Don't cry, Nabila,' Fajr soothed, stroking my face. 'You can come and visit any time you like.'

I was sad to lose a friend and ally, someone I could trust in the house. Maybe it was partly her influence that helped me to stand up for myself and move away from my traditional upbringing to become more modern and daring. I'd had enough of my parents controlling me and telling me what to do all the time. Besides, I didn't want to be the boring old Nabila any more; I wanted to be a new and exciting one who made her own decisions in life.

At the age of fourteen I challenged another taboo. I'd never tasted alcohol before, and to a Muslim it's strictly forbidden, but when a school friend produced a bottle of Bacardi in the local park I decided to have a swig.

Everyone around me gasped. They all knew I wasn't allowed to drink. The silence was broken with laughter. Some friends even patted me on the back in support. I was just the same as them, as I'd always wanted to be.

The Bacardi warmed my throat as it slid down. Soon we were all taking glugs from the bottle, while sitting on the kids' roundabout. It wasn't long before my head felt fuzzy. I liked the numbness but I didn't like the way it made me lose control. I was frightened that I might say something, let something slip about the bad old days in the mosque. I'd die if that happened. I looked around and saw some of the girls and boys were kissing, and I didn't like that either. As quick as a flash it took me back to the dark little bedroom. I could feel the imam's hot breath against my neck, smell his rancid smell in my nostrils, feel the pain as he bit me. I shut my eyes and willed the nasty thoughts to go away.

'You all right?' someone asked.

'Yeah, yeah, I'm fine,' I lied.

But the next time the bottle was passed my way I pursed my lips and just pretended to take another gulp before passing it on. I decided that I'd never get so drunk that I'd lose control. Instead, whenever someone brought booze to the park from then on I'd pretend to be drunk, just so that I'd fit in.

It was around that time I started stealing Mum's make-up. In the end she got so fed up of me taking it that she bought me some of my own. I loved trying out new lipsticks and eye shadows and soon learnt how to apply just the right amount of eyeliner and mascara to emphasise my eyes, making them stand out. Dad didn't like me wearing make-up and at first he forbade it but, as usual, Mum held the most power and she convinced him it was natural for a girl my age to experiment.

'She can wear it as long as she just wears it inside the house when she's with me,' Mum decreed.

At that time she had started work in a clothing factory and often brought home trendy samples of modern British outfits. She offered me a few things and I loved dressing up in them rather than the more modest clothes I normally wore, but I was forbidden from wearing them out of the house. Dad went mad when he saw me in the low-necked blouses and short skirts and made me take them straight off again.

But I was becoming more and more rebellious and the temptation of being able to dress just like my school friends was too much, so I'd often sneak out wearing modern clothes underneath my coat. Once I was safely down in the park, I'd reveal my new look to my friends.

I loved to feel part of the crowd, to be accepted by them as an equal.

When I was fifteen, Dad suddenly announced that I no longer had to marry Fajr's brother. Things had become strained between Fajr and my parents because Dad felt that she was too bossy and ruled my brother with a rod of iron. Despite the fact that he'd given his word, he wanted to get me out of a situation in which I might be bullied by a family with such strong characters and opinions.

'The marriage is off,' he told me one night. 'You will marry, but not yet.'

With that, he walked out of the room. I was dumbfounded and tried to ask Mum why, but neither would go into detail. Still, it meant I was able to choose what I wanted to do when I left school. Instead of getting married straight away, I decided that I wanted to get a job working with children. I hoped I would be able to protect them, the way no one had protected me. The thought that I hadn't spoken out against the imam still plagued me. I was tormented because at the back of my mind was the thought that he could have done this to someone else. If only I'd spoken out then, maybe I could have stopped him.

But everyone had let me down – the imam and my parents. I'd had to fend for myself and I was determined that no other child would suffer as I had. It was my way of making amends, of making peace with my conscience.

'I want to go to college and train to be a nursery nurse,' I told my parents one night over dinner.

'But what about getting married?' Mum asked.

'I want to do something more with my life.'

When I first brought it up Dad refused point blank, but after a couple of weeks of constant nagging he finally changed his mind. Once he had, there was no turning back for me. I was going to college when I left school and that's all there was to it.

'You can only go if I take you there in the morning and pick you up at night, understand?' Dad insisted. He'd heard of Muslim girls going to the local college and dating white boys, then running away from their families, and he didn't want me falling into bad ways.

'Yes, Dad,' I replied, planting a kiss on his forehead. Any hurt I'd felt about the way he'd responded to the news of what the imam did to me had passed. I still felt aggrieved about Mum because she was a woman and should have been the one to protect her daughter, but my dad was a different matter. I was still a daddy's girl at heart. I loved him and wanted to make him proud of me.

School finished and I left with a handful of reasonable grades, then started college the following September. There were only a few of us on the course but it didn't matter – this was exactly what I wanted to do. The course lasted two years and during that time we got to go on placements, working with babies and children under the age of five – it was a dream come true. I loved watching the children grow and develop into happy and confident individuals. At one time I worked in a reception class, where the new arrivals were often upset and crying for their mothers, and I found I had a natural talent for cheering up sad or shy children. When they were happy, some of that happiness transferred back onto me. I loved my career. It brought me a kind of fulfilment that nothing else had done before, as if it was my purpose in life to protect kids.

Despite my promises to Dad that I would behave at college, I was soon rebelling in another way: going through his pockets and stealing his cigarettes. I thought smoking made me look cool, grown-up and sophisticated. It wasn't long before he found out.

'So when did you take up smoking then?' he asked one night as he picked me up.

I racked my brains. Had he seen me? Would he stop me going to college? But he didn't. Even Dad knew that I couldn't be hemmed in any more. I often wondered if the guilt of not acting over the imam had somehow loosened his vice-like grip on me. My parents had turned a blind eye to something as awful as that, so how could they now lecture me about the evils of smoking?

I had my own life and my own dreams – but someone was about to enter it and turn it upside down all over again.

Chapter 24

My Sikh Boyfriend

Life at college was good. I made my own decisions and got to choose my own friends. Dad had to stop picking me up at night because he'd developed diabetes and his eyesight was failing, so the doctor advised him to give up driving. He was heartbroken, but he knew in the long run it was the safest thing to do so he sold his car. I was upset for him, but the knock-on effect was fantastic because I was allowed to catch the bus home alone at night, which meant I could hang around with my friends and have a social life.

On my eighteenth birthday I met some friends in the college café. A few had brought me presents and as I excitedly ripped off the wrapping paper I felt a pair of dark brown eyes watching me from across the room. It was a boy I had spotted before at college, who I thought was very handsome, and now he was watching me. I noticed a bangle on his right arm, just like the ones that

Suki and her brothers had worn. That meant he was Sikh. I felt my heart flutter slightly. I'd always loved our Sikh friends. I thought back to when I was a little girl and had always wanted to be a Sikh. Maybe this was my destiny.

I waved at the boy and he strolled over to chat.

'My name's Guvi,' he smiled. His eyes were warm and kind. Unlike the other Sikhs I'd met, he had short, cropped hair. The bangle on his right arm was the only sign of his religion.

'I'm Nabila,' I answered. 'It's my eighteenth birthday today and we're going to the pub. Do you want to come?'

He couldn't make it that night but the ice was broken. We got talking, and a week later when he asked me out I answered 'yes' straight away.

'Whoa!' Guvi laughed. 'Don't you even want to think about it?'

'Nope,' I grinned back.

The following week was the half-term holiday from college but Guvi had offered to take me on a date to the cinema and I wasn't going to miss it for anything.

'I'm just off to college,' I lied to my parents as I grabbed my bag and rushed out the door.

I was careful to watch out for my brothers on the way. The family wouldn't have accepted me dating any boy, but a Sikh boy was especially taboo because of that crazy old enmity between Muslims and Sikhs. Guvi was already waiting for me as I approached the cinema.

'Hi,' he said, grabbing my hand. 'I've bought our tickets. It's a film called *Mrs Doubtfire*, about a nanny. I thought it'd be right up your street.'

The movie was hilarious and I kept thinking how much fun it was finally to be out on a date. This was how it was meant to be. I was here by choice, not because my parents had arranged it. I felt happy, confident and relaxed in his company. That night, as I went for the bus home, I felt as if I was walking on air. This was the real deal. Guvi was a gentleman – he hadn't even tried to kiss me, just gently held my hand throughout the film. I'd felt safe, happy but, above all, I felt protected by this gorgeous man.

We started seeing each other regularly, and gradually he became more affectionate towards me. One day he slipped his arm around my waist and I immediately thought of the imam's hand snaking around my waist and working its way down to my bum. I shook the thought from my head. Guvi was different. He wasn't the imam.

The first time he kissed me, I shut my eyes and felt our lips touch tenderly. I'd been sure the imam would dominate my thoughts but he didn't, because this kiss was so different from the disgusting licking, sucking and biting he used to do. It was loving, gentle and all I'd ever wanted.

It was the first time I'd been remotely intimate with anyone since the abuse. I'd been scared that the imam had ruined my life for good and that I'd never be happy with a boy, but I was wrong. I loved Guvi and he loved me. That kiss had helped to heal me, and now, for the first time, I felt as though I was winning.

But over the months the kisses became more frequent and led to other things, which weren't quite as easy to cope with.

'Why do you flinch whenever I go near you?' Guvi asked one day.

'It's nothing,' I told him, but he knew there was something wrong.

He put his hand on my breast but I pushed it away.

'What's going on? Don't you like me?' he asked, exasperated.

'No, no, it's not that, it's just …' my voice tailed off. Where on earth would I start?

I didn't want to tell Guvi about the imam but if I didn't then I was in real danger of losing him. I was testing his patience to the limit because every time he placed his hand on my body, trying to coax me to give in to him, a warning noise would implode inside my brain and transport me straight back to the imam's stinking, dark little office. Guvi's hands would become the imam's grubby, groping hands. I thought I had moved on but the reality was that I was far from it.

Soon Christmas was upon us. We'd been dating for six months and Guvi was desperate for us to spend some private time together as a couple.

'I've booked us a room in a hotel,' he announced.

Panic rose up inside me. I knew he'd expect me to go all the way with him, but how could I? I was simply petrified.

That afternoon my heart raced as I walked into the hotel reception to meet him. As we took a lift up to the room it continued to beat so loudly that I thought it might leap out of my chest.

Guvi was determined that nothing would spoil the special moment. We exchanged Christmas presents and he'd bought me some gorgeous boots, my favourite perfume, underwear, a teddy bear and, of course, some Kylie CDs.

Then he began undressing me very slowly, all the time kissing and caressing me. My immediate reaction was to run screaming the other way, but at the same time I enjoyed what he was doing to me. It felt right, good even. Then he led me to the bed and moved his hand up to cup my left breast. As soon as I felt it there I froze and pushed it away.

'I don't believe it! You're doing it again!' he complained. 'Is there someone else? Is that it?'

'No,' I began to sob. 'I promise – I wouldn't do that to you.' This was it – I had to tell him here and now. If I didn't, I'd lose Guvi forever.

I turned and faced the wall as I spoke, tears streaming down my face. 'Something happened to me when I was much younger,' I began.

Guvi wrapped his arms around me. 'I knew it!' he said. 'I knew something was wrong.'

'It happened at the mosque. I was only seven years old ...' I told him about the imam, the abuse, how he bit my cheek, pushed his finger deep inside me. Everything.

Soon I was exhausted. The words had just come spilling out. Once I'd started there was no stopping. It felt wonderful to be able to tell someone, as if all the years of hurt and fear had finally come flooding out. Now I was awash with something new – relief.

When I'd finished, Guvi didn't say very much, but he held me like a baby.

'I'll look after you. I'll protect you. No one will ever hurt you again, understand?'

I nodded, emotionally drained and with no more tears left.

'We'll get a place of our own, then I can protect you forever,' Guvi said, his eyes lighting up at his suggestion.

We didn't have sex that day. Instead we just kissed and cuddled until it was time to go home. It was months after that before we finally made love, and when it happened it felt natural but still it didn't stop the flashbacks. I tried to shake them from my head, but I didn't enjoy sex. I was tense and jumpy and it hurt, just as it had with the imam. Afterwards I was sore and began to bleed.

I'd only had sex with Guvi because it was something I felt I had to do or I would lose him. In my mind, sex wasn't meant to be enjoyed – it was just another chore. Our sex life was continually haunted by my flashbacks. Everything reminded me of the imam and what he'd made me do as a child. Sex was something horrible, nasty and dirty. If I was honest, the whole idea of it turned my stomach.

I was naïve. I thought that I'd forgotten the imam, but he was still there. He was alive and well and living inside my head.

It wasn't long before Mum found out that I had a boyfriend. She'd suspected for ages but I always denied it, then one day she hid outside college and watched us coming out and standing at the bus stop together, his arm around me. Her eagle eyes also spotted his Sikh bracelet and she charged across to confront me.

'How long has this being going on?' she yelled, looking me up and down. 'Let's wait and see what your father has to say about that. This boy's a Sikh, of all things!'

I stared at her, my mouth open in astonishment at her hypocrisy. 'Well,' I threatened, with tears in my eyes, 'if you tell Dad about my boyfriend I'll tell him all about you and Aariz!'

Suddenly Mum went very quiet. I'd knocked the wind from her sails.

'You wouldn't!'

'Try me,' I warned.

We travelled home together and the atmosphere was tense, but Mum didn't say anything to Dad that night. She couldn't risk it.

I was now nineteen years old, and I knew I didn't want a marriage arranged by my parents any more. I wanted to choose my own partner. I wanted Guvi. I just had to find a way of getting Dad to agree – and that was never going to be easy.

But then something happened which turned my whole world upside down. One day I returned from college to find Dad lying on the sofa. He'd felt so ill that he'd come home early from the mosque. Mum was so concerned she phoned for an ambulance, while I got a glass of water for him to sip.

Mum took him into hospital, along with Tariq, who was home on leave from the army. I got in touch with Habib, Saeed and Asif, who all came to the house, and they were there late that night when Mum arrived home with the awful news that Dad had suffered a massive

heart attack and died at the age of fifty-nine. She staggered into the house and collapsed onto the floor where
she wailed like a wounded animal. It took all the boys'
strength just to lift her and carry her to the sofa.

'No!' I sobbed, so grief-stricken that I thought my
heart would rip in two. Despite everything that had
happened to me, and the fact that nothing had been
done about the imam or the abuse, I'd never blamed
Dad. I always felt it was Mum pulling the strings and
that any choices he'd made, rightly or wrongly, he'd
been encouraged to make by her. My father was my
world. He'd made me the person I was as an adult. He'd
instilled in me a kindness and compassion for others.
My life had been made so much richer by knowing and
loving this gentle and wonderful man. He would have
walked to the ends of the earth for us, but now he had
gone I knew my life could never be the same again.

According to Muslim religion, we had to bury the
body as soon as possible. Dad's wish was to be buried
back in Pakistan, along with his mother and his sister.
Mum switched to auto-pilot and started phoning
around, making the arrangements. A couple of days
later, along with my two older brothers, she flew his
body to Pakistan. Asif, Tariq and I were left behind to
mourn alone. I never even got the chance to say goodbye, and the grief hit me hard. Dad's death made me
grow up really quickly. Just as I'd found happiness in
my life, reality came and slapped me around the face.

I never knew whether Mum had told Dad about my
relationship with Guvi, but my brothers found out and
soon enough a family meeting was called. Guvi and I

were summoned to the house, and when we entered the room Mum stood up to face us.

'You've either got to convert to being a Muslim or we're going to kill you,' she threatened.

I was dumbstruck. Was she serious? I looked at my brothers for support but they were all too scared to stand up to Mum. Tariq tried to put in a word for me, but with Dad gone Mum had all the power.

'This is just like a Bollywood film!' Mum snarled at Guvi, sarcastically. 'She thinks she's going to marry you and you'll all live happily ever after, but you won't!'

Guvi looked petrified. I knew he would never convert, so the pressure was on for us to break up. That day things changed in our relationship.

'I don't know whether I can go through with this any more,' Guvi said sadly after we left the house.

I was heartbroken but I couldn't blame him. 'Let's run away together,' I suggested.

'No, Nabila, I'm not running away. It's not the answer.'

Mum increased the pressure on me, saying, 'Your father only had a heart attack and died because he found out you were with a Sikh and he couldn't take the shame. It's your fault. You killed him.'

The words cut deep into my heart and I began to cry. 'But Dad didn't die because of me.'

'Yes, he did – you made him sick with worry and shame and then he had a heart attack and died,' she said, twisting the knife a little further.

I carried the guilt with me constantly. I must have been a complete disappointment for Dad, a million miles away from the good Muslim girl he had wanted for a daughter. I'd never know for sure if she told him or she was just using this as a weapon to threaten me with, but all the worry and stress mixed up with grief made me ill.

Guvi was getting similar pressure from his family and he moved out of home into a flat. It meant we could spend time together more easily, but Mum then asked some old family friends to follow us and intimidate us in an effort to break us apart. By this time I was twenty years old. I'd left college and secured a job as a nanny. Guvi and I were determined to be together and nothing would stop us, but once they found out where Guvi lived, Mum's acquaintances trashed his car, smashing all the windows and scratching the paintwork. It was terrifying. They got hold of his telephone number and rang him at all hours of the day and night, threatening his life. They put us under enormous pressure, but still Guvi and I stuck together.

I would have liked to marry him, but he didn't ask me and I assumed it was because of all the trouble between our families. To get married would mean rubbing salt in the wounds and could have pushed them over the edge once and for all, so we continued as we were. I lived at home with my family but spent as much time as I could at Guvi's flat, and we hoped that our families would come around in the end when they saw that we were still together.

At the age of twenty-three, when I'd been seeing Guvi for five years, Mum called a family meeting at which she announced I was being sent over to Pakistan to get married. None of my brothers stuck up for me – not even Asif, who had umpteen white girlfriends. Mum had decided, and that was that.

I didn't say a word; instead I got up, left the room and went to my bedroom. I felt a numb kind of disbelief that this was happening. I was a grown woman with her own income, yet other people were still trying to make decisions for me. I had no control over my life, just as I'd had no control over the imam or the abuse I'd suffered as a child. But now I'd reached breaking point – I'd had enough. I pulled down a suitcase from the top of the wardrobe and began to pack, then I picked up my mobile, calmly dialled a number and spoke to a friend from work.

'Ali, can you pick me up at the end of my street in five minutes?'

'Of course,' she replied without asking why. She knew what my mother was like.

I took as much as I could carry, then I crept down the stairs and slipped out the front door. As soon as the night air hit my lungs, I started to run as fast as I could down the street. I didn't once stop to look back. Instead I ran to the safety of my friend waiting in her car, and a whole new future.

Chapter 25

New
Beginnings

After leaving home, I moved into Guvi's flat. It should have been the happiest time of my life. I was finally with the man I loved and had walked away from my controlling mother – but it wasn't long before things started to go wrong between us. I could tell that I cramped Guvi's style. He was used to living on his own and didn't really want to live with me. He resented my presence and we began to argue in a way we never had before.

A few weeks after I left home, my brother Tariq came into work to speak to me. As soon as I saw him walking towards me I knew instinctively that something was wrong.

'Nabila, it's Mum,' he began. 'She's taken an overdose.'

The words hit me like a right hook.

'When?' I asked. 'Is she all right?'

'She's in hospital.'

I ran over to my boss and told her that I had to leave immediately, then I grabbed my coat and bag and hurried out to Tariq's car.

'Is she going to live?' I asked, as he started up the engine. 'Why has she done this?'

Tariq looked annoyed. 'Isn't it obvious?' he asked. 'Why won't you just come home, then everything will be all right?'

When he told me the story in the car, I soon realised that Mum hadn't actually planned to die. She'd rung Habib before swallowing some pills and he'd called an ambulance. It was all a dramatic attention-seeking gesture, and I was furious. When Tariq had first told me the news I'd been terrified that we'd lose her, but now I simply felt annoyed. She didn't deserve my concern. She knew exactly what she was doing. This wasn't about her being depressed; this was about control.

When I finally saw her I was so angry that I could have throttled her. She was selfish. After everything I'd been through, she resented me this one happiness. She never stood up for or supported me after she found out about the abuse, and now she was trying to break me up from my boyfriend just because he was Sikh. It made me dig my heels in even more. Now there was no way I was going back home, not after this.

'But look what you've done to me!' she wailed from her hospital bed. 'You've disgraced the family!'

'I'm never coming home again,' I said, then I turned on my heel and walked out of the hospital.

My family were a bunch of hypocrites. Mum had had an affair with Aariz while Dad was still alive, my brothers had gone out with white girls, they drank and smoked, yet I couldn't even choose my own boyfriend. It was one rule for them and another for me. I'd had enough. I'd been bullied by my mother all my life, but not any more.

A couple of months later, Mum took a second overdose. This time her plan backfired, though: the hospital kept her in a psychiatric unit because she was deemed a risk to herself. They wouldn't let her home until someone agreed to move in and look after her. I refused point blank, so in the end Saeed took her to live with his family in London. I was finally free of her and her controlling ways. Now I'd be able to go out and enjoy life.

One day I rolled out of a club in the early hours of the morning looking for a cab. I finally managed to hail one down and climbed into the back seat, then realised the driver was Sab, the boy who'd called me 'Pizza Face' at school, and the son of Aariz, Mum's lover.

'Nabila!' he exclaimed.

'How are you?' I asked.

He told me he had a white girlfriend and that they'd had a baby out of wedlock.

'My family were appalled!' he laughed.

It was good to know I wasn't the only one with a crazy life and a disapproving family.

'I've got a Sikh boyfriend!' I giggled, half expecting him to be shocked.

He suddenly turned to me. 'I know,' he replied, his voice sounding tense. 'Listen, Nabila, you need to be careful which taxi ranks you use from now on.' He started counting off taxi firm names on his fingers.

'Why?' I asked, puzzled. At first I thought it must be something to do with the prices they charged.

'Because if you or your boyfriend ever catches one of them by mistake then they'll take you away.'

His words hit me like a ton of bricks. 'What do you mean?'

It was obvious Sab was uncomfortable, but he felt he had to tell me out of a sense of loyalty. 'They'll kill you, Nabila,' he said bluntly. 'Your mum has put a hit on your life.'

I reeled back in my seat with shock.

'No, you've got it wrong! You're joking, right?'

Only he wasn't. He explained to me that Mum had offered to pay for Guvi and me to be killed. The people concerned were old friends who were in the minicab business, and we'd be taking our lives in our hands if we ever got into one of their cabs. It all sounded rather amateurish and melodramatic to me, but frightening at the same time – and deeply shocking. I knew that Dad would never have approved of Mum's mad behaviour – she was becoming more unbalanced by the day – yet here she was, still able to talk people into doing crazy things for her. How could she, after everything I'd been through? I was stunned, yet a little part of me wasn't surprised. If Mum could attempt to take her own life – twice – to try and tear me away from Guvi, she was capable of anything. She was unbelievable. Yet it was the sheer thought that she'd go this far that I found most shocking – the fact that my life was worthless in her eyes.

I was shaking like a leaf when I stepped out of the cab.

'Look after yourself, Nabila. Watch your back,' Sab said gently.

I went to pay him.

'No need,' he said, putting a hand up to stop me. 'This is on me.'

As the red lights of his cab disappeared off into the night, suddenly I felt very alone and scared. Sab's words haunted me. For the first time in my life I felt as frightened as when I'd been trapped in the imam's room. Now the threat of danger was coming from my very own flesh and blood – my mother.

For the next few months Guvi and I stopped going out in the evenings and we never used taxis any more. As we stepped out of the flat we looked up and down the street, wondering if someone might be lying in wait, but as the months passed and there hadn't been an attack I began to relax. It didn't look as though anything was going to happen. Maybe Mum was getting the message that I wasn't coming back.

I'd possibly been putting my life at risk to be with Guvi but I began to wonder why, because our home life wasn't at all happy. Within a few months of moving into his flat I'd seen a whole new side to him. He was a bully who ordered me around, making me do all the housework, shopping and laundry while he dictated everything about what we ate, what we watched on television and where we went in the evenings. He'd belittle me, making disparaging comments about my clothes. If I didn't instantly do as he said, I'd get a filthy look and a shove in the back. As things deteriorated, there was the occasional slap in the face, or he'd push me into the furniture. Afterwards he was always apologetic and sweet, so I let it go. What choice did I have?

Then I found out he was having an affair, and I was devastated. His betrayal hit me hard, and I blamed myself for it. I still had hang-ups about sex, because of the flashbacks to the abuse I'd suffered at the hands of the imam. I never enjoyed it. If the sex had been better, I believed Guvi wouldn't have cheated on me. It was all my own fault. I felt worthless and depressed, and I started having panic attacks.

One day at work I collapsed without warning. I struggled to breathe and thought I was going to die. My doctor ran a series of tests but they all came back negative, and he said he thought it was a panic attack brought on by stress. He prescribed some medication to calm my nerves, but now I felt as if I was going mad.

The medication calmed the panic attacks but I began to hear voices in my head whenever I got stressed. There were three voices in total – the three people who'd hurt me in life. The imam's voice was loud and clear and would torment me constantly, but I also heard Mum's and Guvi's voices telling me how worthless and useless I was. I tried to shake them from my head but whenever I had doubts the voices would come back to haunt me.

I felt as though I was losing my mind. I thought I'd dealt with the abuse years ago. I'd buried it deep down inside, yet here it was, trying to surface again. I'd tried to push the flashbacks out of my mind but they'd refused to stay away. I wondered whether it was my conscience haunting me because I'd never spoken out against the imam. Maybe that was it. Like a coward, I'd slipped away, leaving him free to abuse more children in his care. I wondered if there had been other victims like me. Deep down, I suspected there probably had been. I'd had the power to stop that from happening, but I'd been too much of a coward. Now the guilt was coming back to haunt me, and this time it was driving me slowly insane.

In a desperate bid to stop the voices I decided to get away for good and applied for a series of jobs miles away from home. To my delight, I was offered a job in London, but when Guvi found out about it he begged me not to go.

'Nabila, I don't want you to leave,' he begged. 'I've made the biggest mistake of my life. I'll change, I promise. Please give me another chance.'

He convinced me that he had broken up with the girl concerned and that it had only been a one-off anyway, and like a fool I believed him. I convinced myself that things would be different from now on.

But despite Guvi's promises, things didn't improve; in fact, they got worse. He'd arrive home later and later each night. He'd tell me that he'd been out with mates from work but his breath never smelled of alcohol. I knew he was lying, so one evening I demanded to know where he'd been.

'Your dinner is cold. It was ready hours ago but you didn't come home. I don't believe you've been with people from work. I want to know what's going on. You're back with her, aren't you?'

I expected excuses but it came like a bolt out of the blue: a sharp stinging pain to the side of my face. Guvi had punched me, hard. At first the shock rather than the pain left me reeling. I burst into tears.

Guvi was horrified. 'Nabila, I'm so sorry. I promise this will never happen again.'

'You just hit me,' I said, trembling. 'I can't believe it; you just hit me.' That was all I could muster.

Afterwards I looked into the mirror and noticed a purplish bruise beginning to form on the side of my cheek. It reminded me of the dirty love bites that the imam had given me all those years before and in my head it took me straight back to those times.

After Guvi had crossed the line, there was no going back. Soon he was frequently lashing out at me in temper, especially if I questioned where he had been. He was careful to whack me in the stomach or on the back, where the bruises would be hidden. Sometimes he'd grip the tops of my arms and squeeze them hard until I felt as though they would snap like twigs. But I was already broken, in more ways than one. I considered leaving him but I had nowhere to go. This was my bed and I'd have to lie in it and suffer the consequences of my actions. Maybe it was all I deserved. I'd always felt worthless, and this confirmed it.

The look on his face as he attacked me often reminded me of the sick look on the imam's face when he beat Hamal. He became twisted and evil. I thought I'd moved on with my life, but as I lay on the floor after yet another beating I realised that I hadn't at all. I was still a victim. Instead of the imam, Guvi was my abuser. I'd been transported back to being a frightened little girl again.

I was simply terrified of Guvi, so much so that when he talked me into buying a home with him I was too frightened to say no. I was scared of him and he knew it. But he was also very clever and kept all the legal documents in his name. I paid half of the bills but it was his name on the deeds to the house. It was supposed to be a new start, but after his affair and the physical violence things were never the same again. The trust had gone.

At the age of twenty-eight, I'd been with Guvi for ten years but I wasn't happy. I was paranoid all the time. Life was miserable. And then one night as I walked home, a motorbike pulled out of nowhere, I felt a sharp pain in my leg and everything went black. I woke up in a bright white room. At first I thought I was dead, but then I noticed a nurse hovering over me and realised I was in a hospital bed.

'Nabila, you've been knocked over,' the nurse said. 'Your leg was badly broken so you've had to have an operation.'

My head felt heavy and woozy, and the words floated in and out of my consciousness. Leg. Broken. Operation.

When I awoke again, I found my family crowded around my bedside. My leg had been so badly shattered that doctors had had to pin it back together. It was swollen and swathed in bandages. I thought how ironic it was that after all those years when I sliced and scarred my legs to ribbons, now I had the mother of all scars and I hadn't caused it myself.

I was kept in for a week and Guvi came to visit me a couple of times, but he barely spoke and I knew something was wrong. He wasn't even trying to be a loving partner to me. When I got home I listened to some messages on his mobile and my suspicions were confirmed: he was having another affair. In fact, when I confronted him he finally admitted something even more distressing. He told me that a white girl he'd had an affair with some time before had just given birth to his daughter. All the time I'd been paranoid and suspicious, it seemed my suspicions had been completely justified. If only I'd had a modicum of self-esteem I'd have left him years before, but deep down I felt as though I didn't deserve any better. I was worthless, useless, of no value to anyone.

I packed a bag and went to live with Tariq. Guvi begged me to come back, but how could I return to him after the revelation about the child? And just when I thought things couldn't get any worse, I got a phone call from Saeed's wife to tell me that Mum was dying of cancer.

At this stage I hadn't seen Mum for five years but I knew that she had got married down in London, to an imam no less. It felt like the ultimate betrayal. Mum knew what I'd been through at the hands of an imam, but still she was happy to marry one. I didn't trust any of them and felt sick at the thought of one of them being my stepfather. I didn't want to see Mum again. How could I, after finding out she had arranged a hit on me? Besides, I strongly suspected that she had invented the cancer as yet another attention-seeking story, like the suicide attempts.

'No, she's really sick, Nabila,' Saeed's wife told me. 'You need to get down here quickly. It's not a lie. Your mum is dying and she's asking for you.'

Eventually she persuaded me to come to London for a visit, but I was very apprehensive. Was this merely going to give Mum one last chance to kick me in the teeth?

When I walked into her hospital room, I staggered in shock. My beautiful mum was lying there, gaunt and ill, with a sickly grey pallor. She'd lost all her beautiful long hair. As soon as she saw me her dark eyes widened.

'Nabila,' she cried, holding out her arms, 'is it really you?'

'Yes, Mum,' I said, cradling her. 'Don't worry, I'm here now.'

Straight away I knew I'd done the right thing. Mum was obviously dying and this would be our only chance to make amends. As I held her, I could feel her bones jutting out, digging into the undersides of my arms. She was as fragile as a tiny bird. We were both crying.

'I'm so happy you're here,' she whispered.

'So am I,' I said, and I meant every word. Despite everything that had happened between us, I knew it was important to be there for her. I did love her deep down, and now it seemed we had very little time left. Life was too short for bitterness.

I was so caught up with emotion that I hardly noticed the strange man sitting in the corner of the room.

'This is my daughter,' Mum called over him. 'Isn't she beautiful?'

I realised he must be her new husband, the imam. He studied me for a moment before smiling warmly. My stomach lurched and I felt my flesh crawl. It wasn't his fault – I'd never met him before – but he looked OK. It

was the fact he was an imam that bothered me. I hadn't
gone inside a mosque or been in the company of an
imam since I'd escaped from one at the age of eleven.

'Hello,' he said, stretching his hand out to me. 'I'm
your dad.'

'No, you're not!' I snapped, a little too harshly. 'My
father's dead!'

Mum shook her head as if to say, 'Here we go again.'
The imam tutted and gave me a judgemental look. I
didn't care. I neither sought nor needed his approval; I
was here for my dying mum and that's all that mattered.

A little later the morphine took hold and she fell into
a deep sleep. Now it was just me and him in the room.

'You should pray,' he insisted. 'Do you pray?'

Without looking at him, I raised my hand to stop the
conversation. 'Don't, just don't,' I hissed. 'Don't even
bother to lecture me because I'm not interested.'

I wasn't a little girl any more. I didn't have to listen
to the imam, or any man for that matter. I could make
up my own mind about what I wanted to do from now
on.

We didn't speak again. His influence on my mother
was apparent, as she'd suddenly become very religious.
I didn't know if it was down to her new marriage or the
fact that she'd been diagnosed with terminal cancer but,
whatever the reason, I didn't like it. It seemed all wrong
after everything I'd been through at the mosque.

She was transferred to a hospice and I sat by her
bedside for ten days. The airless little room became my
prison as I watched her fade away before my eyes. One
by one my brothers arrived until there was no space

left. Thankfully, we were all with her when she died at
the age of just fifty-three.

When I lost Mum, I felt a big empty void in my life.
We'd never seen eye to eye, but I still loved her, and
when she was gone I missed her dreadfully. At the end
of her life I forgave her for everything she'd done to me
– the threat to my life, not supporting me over the
abuse, even her affair. I realised now I was older that
my mother was only human too. She'd made mistakes
as we all do, but deep down everything she'd ever done
had been to protect our family. It wasn't right – but it
didn't make her a bad person.

Chapter 26

Starting Again

Mum's death shook me to the core. Suddenly I felt vulnerable again. News travelled fast and it wasn't long before Guvi was on the phone. I should have hated him but in fact I felt relieved to hear his familiar voice. I suppose Mum's death had made me reassess my own life and I remembered how much I used to be in love with him.

Before long I moved back in with him again, and he brought his little daughter to meet me. I found out that she had been born when I was laid up in hospital with a shattered leg after the motorbike accident. Now I knew everything – there were no more secrets. When I finally saw her, my heart ached. I couldn't believe how beautiful she was. How could I hate this child? But at the same time she reminded me of everything I didn't have. I'd have loved to have a child with Guvi, but he had never agreed to marry me and I wouldn't have wanted a child born out of wedlock.

The day after I met Guvi's daughter, the voices in my head started again. I heard the imam speak to me, then Mum and Guvi: '*You're worthless, you're no good, what a stupid girl.*'

Finally, I was at rock bottom and I decided to kill myself. I dragged myself out of bed and went through every cupboard in the house, emptying all the tablets I could find onto the kitchen table. It was the only way to stop the voices and the torment. I sat at the table with a bottle of vodka and the dozens of pills. I could hear the clock ticking but I've got no idea how long I sat there, clutching my head, trying to stop the voices.

But I couldn't do it – I couldn't even kill myself properly. I sat and looked at the vodka and pills but didn't take any of them. Had Mum felt this desperate when she'd tried to kill herself? Had I made her feel that low? I put the tablets away but I couldn't shake off the hurt and anger I felt inside.

Depression set in once more. I was fast approaching thirty years old and my biological clock was ticking, yet every time I saw a child in the street I'd look away. The constant torment sent me mad. It picked away at me as if it was picking at an open sore. Guvi had a child with someone else, not me. Now other people's children were a constant reminder. I couldn't even bear to work with children any more. I needed a change of career, but I couldn't think what else to do.

Then I remembered. All through my life my looks had made me stand out and got me noticed. I'd spent a lifetime being told how pretty I was; now it was time to use my looks, but this time I'd use them for myself. I visited a model agency and was offered promotional work. The jobs came flooding in. Soon my new career was taking off and I bought my own car. My confidence soared, but Guvi didn't like the new me. He hated my new circle of friends, my clothes and lifestyle. The more he disapproved, the more it spurred me on. I was leaving him behind.

One day I was working with another girl on a promotions job and she told me that she worked as an extra on film and TV sets.

'Wow!' I said, my eyes wide with excitement. 'That sounds really interesting.'

'Hey, you should do it!' she said. 'They're crying out for Asian girls.'

She scrawled a number on a piece of paper and gave it to me.

'You must call them, promise.'

'I promise.'

My hands were shaking as I dialled the number the following morning. I thought of the imam, of Guvi, and all those people who'd told me I was useless. Maybe they'd been right, maybe I *was* useless. I thought no one else would want me – but I was wrong, and soon the TV extra work was flooding in. I was always the girl in the background, but I didn't mind; in fact, I preferred it that way. I liked to blend in. I didn't want to stand out from the crowd any more.

As well as the TV work, I started doing promotions for a radio station. Although it was never going to make me rich, finally I felt as though I belonged. I'd become a different person. Now I was strong and I didn't need Guvi any more. At the age of thirty-one, after thirteen years as his girlfriend, I finally packed my bags and left him to embark on a whole new life.

I felt empowered. I could do this. Now I was the one calling the shots. All those years, all that waiting, and at last I was free to live life on my own terms. At last everything was coming together. Everything was on the up. Not only was I stronger physically, but I was stronger mentally too. I lost all the money I'd ploughed into Guvi's house because of the papers he'd cleverly got me to sign, but I was still able to buy myself a small terraced house. It wasn't very big but I didn't care because it was all mine.

One morning I was called in to a TV studio to work on a drama series. There were dozens of other extras just like me, so at first I didn't notice a young white man with fair hair sitting quietly in the corner. His name was Robert.

We were filming a party scene and the character Robert was playing needed a wife. Without hesitation, he turned and pointed at me.

'How about her?' he said, beckoning me over.

I was uncomfortable with the thought of being in the spotlight but, sick with nerves, I painted on my brightest smile and walked over.

The filming only took minutes, but from that moment on I became Robert's 'wife' for the duration of the series.

'Thanks,' I said to him afterwards.

'No worries. At least you'll get more work!'

We started chatting, and before long we were spending most of our time together, both on set and off. For me it was strictly platonic, but I was intrigued by him. He was a talented actor, and the more we worked together the more I felt drawn to him. He told me he was in a relationship that had hit the rocks. For my part I was terrified of falling in love and getting hurt again, but somehow over the course of several months I came to trust him. I realised he was falling for me as well, and at last he broke up with his girlfriend and we became a couple.

Our relationship was wonderful. I planned to play it cool at first, but things developed really quickly and Robert moved in with me after just a month. However, as soon as we became intimate the old feelings overtook me. I felt dirty and soiled by the imam, even after all this time. The abuse had left me feeling rotten inside, as if I wasn't good enough for Robert, or for any man.

It wasn't long before I began to push Robert away, just as I had with Guvi. He was hurt and confused. He didn't understand, but I didn't want to explain. I was sick of trying to explain, and instead I got angry.

'I don't need another man,' I screamed. 'I'm sick of being controlled by men. Perhaps it would be better if you left.'

My outbursts became more and more frequent, but Robert just sat and took them, one after the other, until one day he said, 'Please tell me what I've done wrong. Why are you always so angry with me?'

'I don't know,' I wailed. 'I don't know why I'm so angry all the time.'

With that I broke down. I wasn't angry with Robert. The truth was, I was still angry with the imam. I was thirty-two years old but I'd never come to terms with what had happened to me inside that mosque between the ages of seven and eleven. Instead, I'd kept my emotions locked away out of sight. I knew they were in there but I didn't want to look at them or deal with them. If I dealt with them, then it would only bring it all back again. But I knew I had to tell Robert or face the prospect of losing him.

'It happened years ago …' I began in a shaky voice. 'I was seven years old. He was a grown man, married with children of his own. He was the imam, the leader of the mosque and of the community. No one would've believed me so I said nothing. I didn't tell a soul. I was frightened and kept it quiet. I suffered in silence night after night as he abused me …'

Robert's eyes widened with horror as he listened. I explained that my parents had found out but had done nothing. I told him how the imam had got away with it for all those years – and the guilt I felt knowing that others might have suffered because of my silence.

'So where is he now?' he finally asked.

I shrugged my shoulders. 'Don't know, but I assume he must be dead by now – it was so long ago.'

'I think you need help to work this all through,' he said when I had finished. 'Have you ever thought of seeing a counsellor?'

I shook my head. There was no way I could tell a complete stranger about the imam.

'It might help,' Robert reasoned.

But I was adamant. It was just too horrible to contemplate. Besides, I was fine now. I'd survived all these years. Why would it help me to talk to a stranger now?

As the months dragged by, I thought more about what Robert had said. I supposed it made sense. One day I wanted us to get married and have kids of our own, but what if my past turned me into a horribly over-protective mum? I couldn't bear to let my abuse ruin my own children's life. He was right; I had to put a stop to this once and for all.

The counsellor I found, a woman, was tremendous. It was hard telling her at first, but once she knew what had happened to me I really started to open up and tell her stuff. It was as if the floodgates had been flung wide open. Everything came pouring out of me: the abuse by the imam, the self-harming, my anger towards my parents but also my grief over losing them, Guvi's violence and betrayal, and my chronically low self-esteem.

I learned to look back as an adult and understand that my parents weren't bad people. They probably thought the imam had only touched me inappropriately on top of my clothes, as he'd done to Wafa, and never had any idea of the full horrific extent of what I went through. By keeping it quiet they felt they were protecting me, so my chances of making a good marriage wouldn't be ruined forever.

Mum was undoubtedly the stronger personality in their marriage and Dad was led by her example, but she'd had a difficult upbringing in which she hadn't known much love, so when she had five children of her own she wasn't able to show love. She was good at the practical things, such as cooking meals and making clothes, but she wasn't a loving mother. That's why I struggled with accepting that anyone loved me as an adult. That's why I didn't feel I was worth it. And it was my low self-esteem that had led me into an abusive relationship with Guvi, one that mirrored the way I felt about myself. After all these years I was still punishing myself for what happened back in the mosque, only now it was emotional punishment rather than cuts with a razor.

The counsellor was fantastic. I underwent regular sessions from then on and they helped me enormously.

'I wish I'd met you years ago,' I told her, my eyes brimming with tears. Robert had been right, I'd needed to do it and now it'd turned out to be the best decision I'd ever made.

Before I left counselling, we discussed whether I should go and report the abuse to the police now.

'He'll either be dead or he'll be living back in Bangladesh, so there's very little point,' I said. 'It's too late.'

All the same, we went through the positive and negative aspects of reporting the abuse. I really wanted to do it, just to have it on record, but at the same time it seemed too daunting. I wasn't sure if I was strong enough to take this any further.

I hadn't realised it, but the fact that my parents didn't support me over the abuse all those years before had taken its toll. One side effect was that I couldn't face rejection, and I was scared that if I went to the police one or all of my brothers would turn away from me. Also, I'd thought the threat to my life over my relationship with Guvi had been the worst danger I faced, but that would be nothing compared to the danger I'd face if I took on such a respected member of the Muslim community. They would be up in arms.

I realised that the prospect of the imam getting a criminal conviction was very unlikely after all this time. If they found him, he was bound to deny everything and it would be his word against mine. Any evidence would be long gone. The only way he could be punished would be if he either admitted it, which wasn't going to happen, or if other girls he had abused came forward. Was that possible?

My old fear of not being believed came to the forefront. But the counsellor believed me, Robert believed me, and when I tearfully told my best friend Jenny about it she believed me straight away.

'Oh my god, Nabila,' she said, wrapping her arms around me. 'Why on earth didn't you tell me before?'

'Because I didn't want it to change our friendship,' I sobbed.

Jenny shook her head firmly. 'Of course it won't!'

I dabbed at my tears with a soggy tissue. 'It's just that so far it's managed to ruin everything else in my life.'

'Come here,' she soothed, hugging me tight.

One night, only weeks after I finished counselling, Jenny and I were driving to visit a friend who'd just returned from a holiday. That night the traffic in the town centre was heavy so we took a different route down some side streets. As we drove along the road I spotted a familiar figure, and the blood drained from my face.

It couldn't be true. He was dead, wasn't he?

I clenched my fists tight in my lap and my heart began to pound.

It was more than twenty years since I'd last seen him and he was much older but it was definitely him. I'd have recognised that grotesque pot belly anywhere. I looked again, just to be sure. He wasn't wearing a sarong; instead he wore trousers, a long shirt and jacket, but he looked very unkempt as he waddled along. He was as filthy and disgusting as I'd remembered. I wanted Jenny to mow him down right there and then, to kill him on the pavement. He was sauntering along, looking as if he didn't have a care in the world.

'Oh my god!' I screamed.

Jenny panicked and, thinking there must be something in the middle of the road, she hit the brakes and did an emergency stop. The tyres screeched against the tarmac as the car skidded to a halt. The sound made the imam turn back momentarily and look over his shoulder towards us. I saw him in the wing mirror, and suddenly I was a frightened little girl again. What if he came to get me? What if he snatched me from the car and hurt me?

'*Breathe*,' I told myself. '*Remember to breathe.*'

'Nabila, what's the matter?' Jenny demanded. 'You look as if you've just seen a ghost.'

'That's him! That's him!' I babbled.

'Who?' Jenny said, trying to calm me. 'Who is it?'

'You're right,' I told her, aware I wasn't making much sense. 'You're right; I *have* just seen a ghost. It was him, Jenny. That was the imam – the one who abused me.'

'Oh my god! Where? Where is he?' She span around in her seat.

I looked in the wing mirror, but he'd gone.

'Are you sure it was him?'

'Definitely. I'd know him anywhere.' My voice cracked and suddenly I began to cry. Deep sobs welled up inside me. I couldn't help myself. He was alive, he was out there and he could still hurt me.

Jenny wrapped her arms around me. 'What do you want me to do?' she asked.

'I don't know, Jen. Just drive, please. Let's get out of here.'

Robert had gone to London on a business trip but I knew I couldn't face being on my own that night so I texted him and asked him to come back. It was the early hours of the morning when he walked through the door, and he was horrified by my news.

'Right,' he said, running his hands through his hair, 'he's still here. You've got to take action, Nabila. You've got to deal with this once and for all.'

Why was this happening to me now? In all the years since I'd left the mosque I'd never clapped eyes on the man, but here he was less than five miles from my front door.

The imam was living and breathing – he was still a risk to children. I knew I had to do something and do it now.

For several weeks after that I drove around the area, determined to find the bastard. I vowed to hunt him down until he was out in the open, blinking and frightened in the daylight. My quest soon turned into an obsession. I drove along all the side and main roads in the area. I sat in my car for hours at a time, watching and waiting. Now I was the hunter and he was the hunted. The best part was that he didn't even know I was looking for him.

I walked along the same street that Jenny and I had driven down. I peered inside every window to try and catch a glimpse of him. Now our roles were reversed. I needed to find out where he lived so that I could lead the police to his front door and get justice. The urge to find him burned inside me like a secret thread. The longer it took, the more it hurt. But now I wanted to find him, I couldn't. It was impossible, as if he'd simply disappeared off the face of the earth. I was so fired up that I daydreamed about returning to the mosque, barging through the door and demanding to know his whereabouts. However, the thought of actually going near the place made me feel physically ill, so Robert went instead.

It was a warm spring day when he walked in through the mosque door. I told him to remove his shoes before continuing into the old hall. He was there to find things out, but we had to be careful. He couldn't afford to anger the elders. He had to show respect.

Robert approached a man and asked him about the imam who had worked there during the years in question, but he drew a blank. The man simply didn't know.

He said the imam was probably long gone. Only Robert and I knew the truth. But with nothing to go on, our search would have to end there.

He returned home and broke the disappointing news to me. I was annoyed with myself that I hadn't got Jenny to follow him when I saw him. We could have found out where he lived. I needed to know now.

For all those years I'd convinced myself that he was dead, that he couldn't hurt anyone any more, but I'd been wrong. He was very much alive, and the thought of him living and breathing in the same town made my flesh crawl. I wondered how many other children he'd abused since me. Yet again I cursed myself for not speaking out sooner. The guilt weighed heavy on my heart.

I realised that I needed to have my voice heard in order to reach out to those other children, now grown adults, who were still suffering, as I had done. I had to give them a voice; I had to help give them the courage to speak out.

The sun was high in the sky as I walked up the concrete steps of the police station a few days later. For a moment I gripped the metal handrail to steady myself, both mentally and physically.

Robert touched my arm. 'Are you sure you want to do this?'

'Yes,' I replied, my words barely a whisper. 'I'm ready.'

The police station was busy but Robert joined the queue until it was his turn at the front desk. He spoke in a low and quiet voice to the officer, who glanced over at me and nodded.

Moments later a door opened and a female police officer called out my name. I stood up, and after one last look at Robert I walked towards her. It was time.

The room was small and cosy but I still felt very exposed and vulnerable. I began to cry but nothing could stop me telling my story. It had taken so much for me to come this far that there was no going back now.

'I was just seven years old when I started at the mosque,' I began, my voice trembling with emotion. 'He was my religious teacher. I should have been able to trust him … but he made me do unspeakable things …' My voice trailed off to a whisper and then more tears came.

I'd done it, I'd told the police. I'd carried my secret for an agonising twenty-eight years, but now it was over – the secret wasn't mine to keep any longer.

I don't know if justice will be done; I don't know if the police will find him. But I had to tell, not just for me but for all the countless other children who are still too frightened to speak out.

Robert and I plan to get married. It's been a tough journey but I feel as though I've reached the end and now I'm on a different path. We want to have children and I want my kids to be proud of me. I want them to know I am the mum who spoke out against the most powerful man in the Muslim community.

That's why I've written this book. I want my story to be in the public domain because, by speaking about it, we can stop child abuse from happening within all families and all communities.

The Muslim community is a particularly tight-knit one and it's closed off to outsiders, which makes it easier to keep secrets. Family pride is everything, which is why the abuse I suffered was swept under the carpet by my own parents. They were scared of the disgrace it would bring upon them, scared that we'd be outcasts. But I'd rather be an outcast than carry the shame of hiding a paedophile.

I refuse to be silenced any longer. I needed to find my voice and, finally, here it is.

Writing this book has been a therapeutic experience; it's helped me come to terms with everything I've been through. No longer am I seven-year-old Nabila, the frightened little child who thought no one would believe her. I'm stronger than the imam now. For many years I was the victim, but not any more.

I've spoken out not only for myself, but for the countless others out there who can't or who are too frightened to. I dedicate this book to them.

Acknowledgements

I'd like to thank my four brothers. I love you all from the bottom of my heart.

I'd also like to thank my best friend Jenny for her encouragement and, of course, Robert for his continued love and support.

Finally, to other victims of child abuse, please do not suffer in silence – speak out now. I dedicate this book to you.